THE COMPLETE BOOK OF
PHONICS

School Specialty
Children's Publishing

Send all inquiries to:
School Specialty Children's Publishing
8720 Orion Place
Columbus, OH 43240-2111

ISBN 1-56189-207-6

9 10 11 12 13 14 POH 10 09 08 07 06 05 04

Table of Contents

To Parents: The McGraw-Hill Children's Publishing <u>Phonics</u> series emphasizes the key phonics skills that children need to know as they learn to become independent readers. Lessons involve children in the process of reading, writing, listening, and speaking. Children learn to recognize frequently occurring initial and final consonant sounds, and they are introduced to initial and medial short vowel sounds. Creative activities guide children in the blending of sounds and in exploring familiar sound patterns. Additional literature and helpful suggestions further enhance and cultivate children's appreciation of reading.

Phonics Grade K

Phonics Grade 1

Phonics Grade 2

Test Preparation Guide

Phonics Answer Key

Name: _____

Beginning Consonant Bb

The <u>b</u>aby wants to <u>b</u>ounce the <u>b</u>all.

B b   <u>b</u>all

Directions: Say each picture name. If the picture name begins with the same sound as **ball**, color the space.

Can the baby bounce the big beach ball? Could you bounce it? What are some things you can do now that you couldn't do when you were a baby?

Name: _____

Beginning Consonant Cc

<u>C</u>ody <u>C</u>aterpillar needs a warm, <u>c</u>ozy <u>c</u>oat.

C c   <u>c</u>aterpillar

Directions: Cut out the pictures at the bottom. Say each picture name. If the picture name begins with the same sound as **caterpillar**, paste it on Cody to make him a new coat.

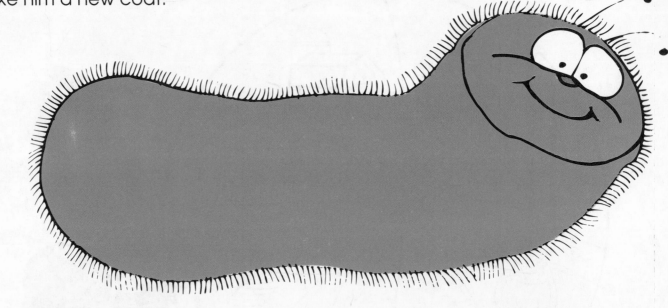

Cocoa and cookies, cuddling your cat . . . What makes you feel warm and cozy?

Beginning Consonant Tt

<u>T</u>ommy put <u>t</u>oo many <u>t</u>oys in the <u>t</u>ub.

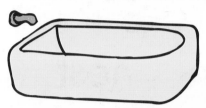

T t   <u>t</u>ub

Directions: Say the picture name for each toy in the tub. If the picture name begins with the same sound as **tub**, mark an X on it.

What are your favorite tub toys?

Beginning Consonant Nn

The sleepy baby birds want to <u>n</u>ap in their <u>n</u>est.

N n   <u>n</u>est

Directions: Help the birds find their nest. Follow the path with the pictures whose names begin with the same sound as **nest**.

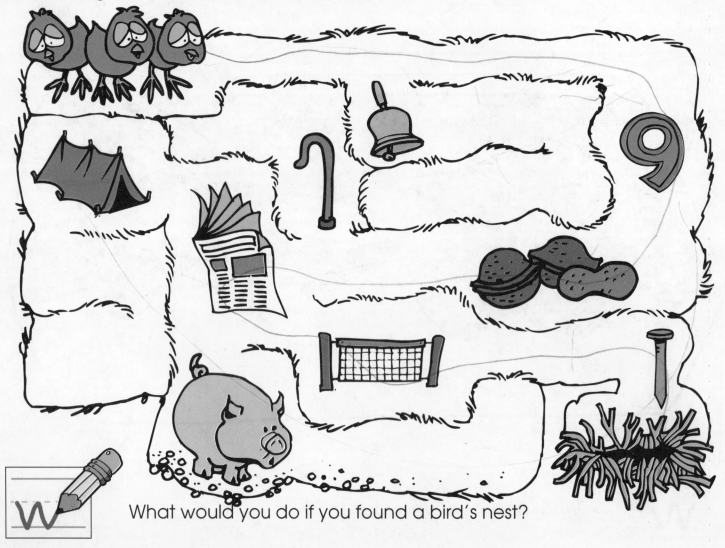

What would you do if you found a bird's nest?

Name: _____

Beginning Consonant Pp

Pam packs her panda for a sleepover.

P p   panda

Directions: Pam only packs things whose names begin with the same sound as **panda**. What else will she pack? Say the picture names. Draw a line from Pam to each picture whose name begins with the same sound as **Pam** and **panda**.

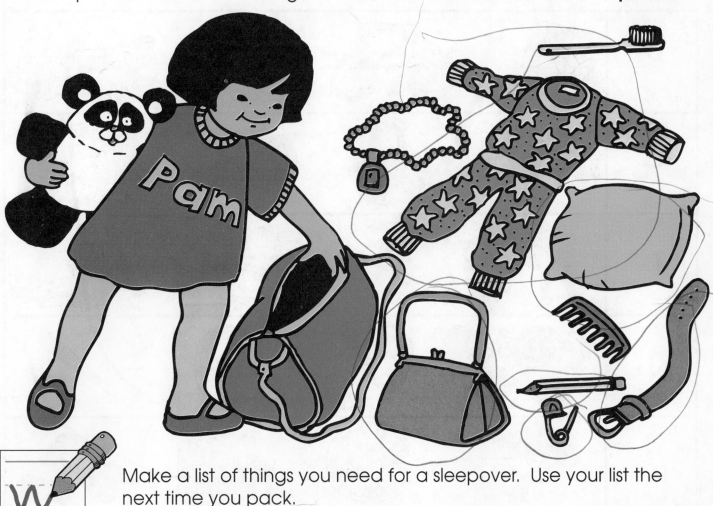

Make a list of things you need for a sleepover. Use your list the next time you pack.

Name: _____

Review Beginning Consonants

B b   **C c**   **T t**   **N n**   **P p**

Directions: Look at the letter at the beginning of each row. Then say each picture name. Circle each picture whose name begins with the sound the letter stands for.

Name: _____

Review Beginning Consonants

Directions: Say each picture name. Circle the letter that stands for the beginning sound.

(P) T	(B) P	N (C)	B (T)
(N) B	T (N)	T (B)	T (P)
(P) B	(C) P	C (B)	T (C)
(T) P	(N) C	N (P)	B (P)
(B) C	P (N)	(C) B	C (T)

Name: _____

Ending Consonants

Directions: Say each picture name. Fill in the circle next to the letter that stands for the **last** sound.

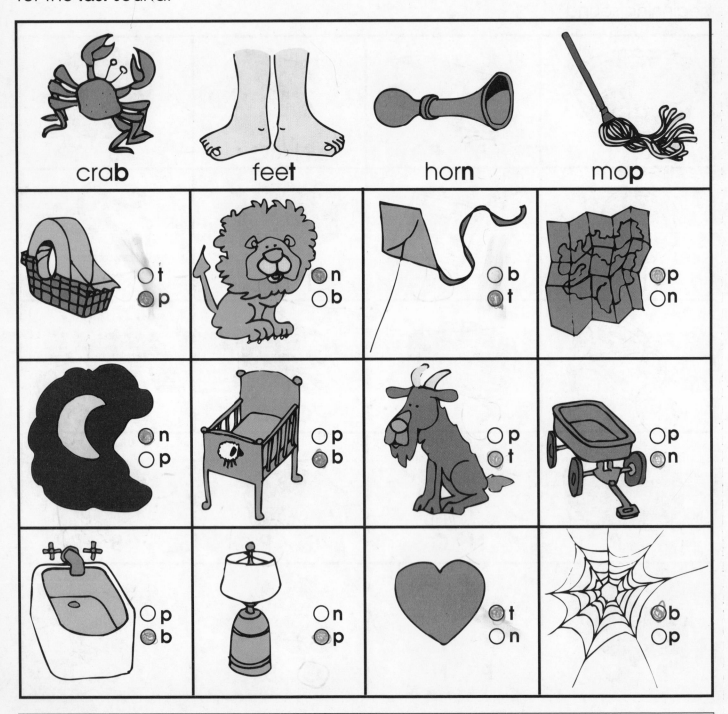

cra**b**   fee**t**   hor**n**   mo**p**

○ t   ○ n   ○ b   ○ p
● p   ○ b   ● t   ○ n

● n   ○ p   ○ p   ○ p
○ p   ● b   ● t   ○ n

○ p   ○ n   ● t   ● b
● b   ● p   ○ n   ○ p

Name: _____

Rhyming Words

The busy <u>man</u> pours the soup from the <u>can</u> into the <u>pan</u>.

Directions: Words that have the same ending sounds, like **man** and **pan**, are called **rhyming words**. Say the names of the pictures. In each box circle the pictures that have rhyming names.

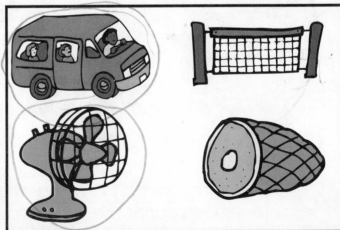

Name: _____

Short Vowel a

The b<u>a</u>nd of <u>a</u>nts play r<u>a</u>t-<u>a</u>-t<u>a</u>t-t<u>a</u>t!

<u>a</u>nts

Directions: Short **a** is the sound you hear at the beginning of the word **ants**. Only animals whose names have the **short a** sound can play in the ants' band. Say each picture name. Circle the picture if you hear the **short a** sound.

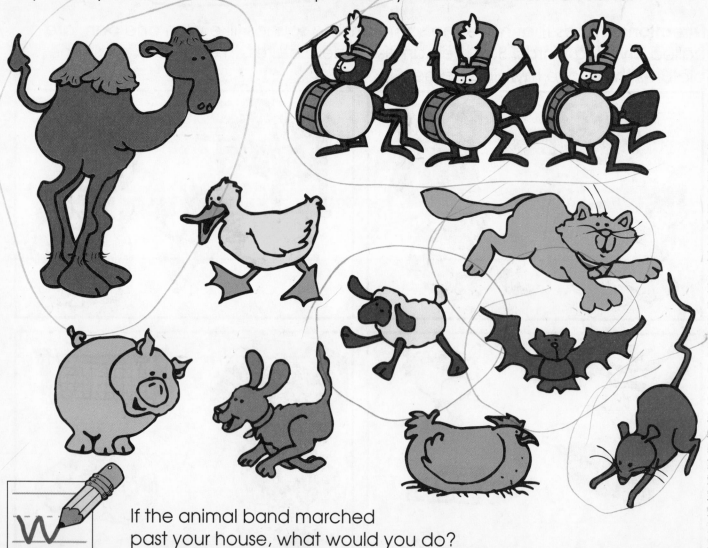

If the animal band marched past your house, what would you do?

Name: _____

Short Vowel a

Directions: Say each picture name. Write **a** if you hear the **short a** sound.

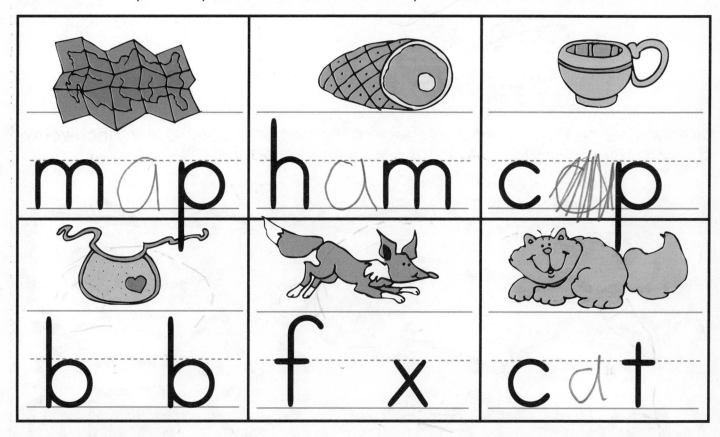

m a p   h a m   c a p

b b   f x   c a t

Directions: Use a toy car or pretend your finger is a car at the top of each hill. Smoothly move your finger or car down the hill as you blend the letter sounds to say the name of the picture. Then trace its name on the line.

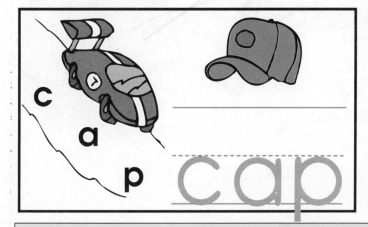

c a p   cap

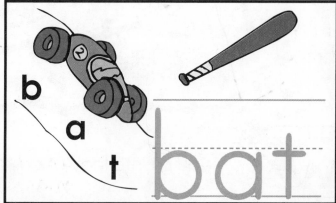

b a t   bat

aeiou

Name: _____

Short Vowel i

Help Iggy Inchworm crawl around the twigs to his home.

inchworm

Directions: Short **i** is the sound you hear at the beginning of the word **inchworm**. Say each picture name. Follow the path with the pictures whose names have the **short i** sound.

If you bit into Iggy's house, what would Iggy say to you?

Name: _____

Short Vowel i

Directions: Use a toy car or your finger to smoothly blend the letter sounds to read each word. Write the word on the line.

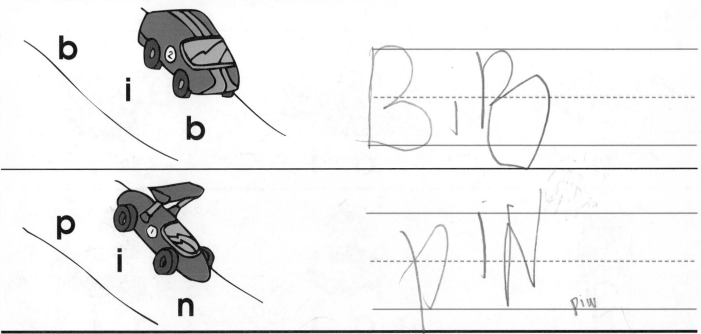

BiB

PiN

piw

Directions: Write the word from above that names each picture. Then find three other things in the picture whose names have the short i sound and circle them.

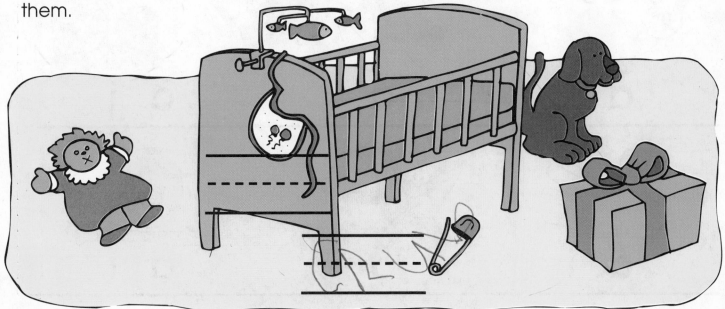

Review Short Vowels a and i

Directions: Say each picture name. Circle the letter that stands for the **vowel sound** you hear.

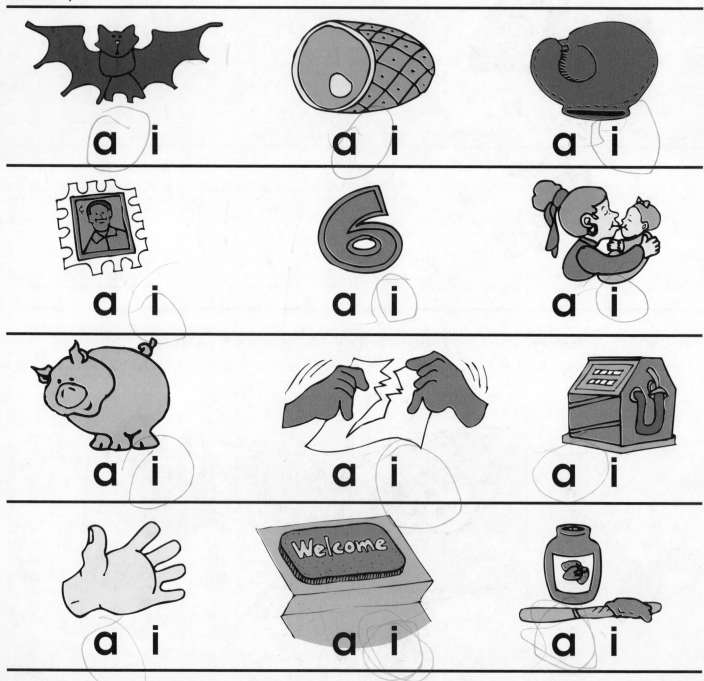

Name: _____

Beginning Consonant Hh

Raise your <u>h</u>and and wave <u>h</u>ello!

H h   <u>h</u>and

Directions: Say each picture name. If the picture name begins with the same sound as **hand**, color the bead.

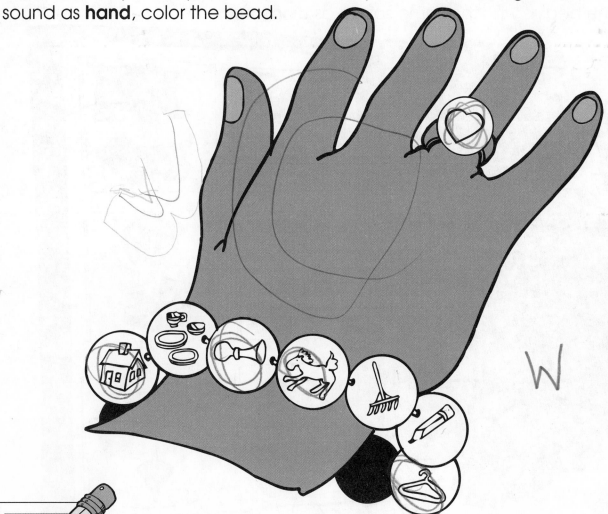

How would you say hello to someone who speaks another language?

Beginning Consonant Dd

Oh, no! A <u>d</u>inosaur is at the <u>d</u>oor!

D d <u>d</u>inosaur

Directions: Say the picture names in each box on the door. Circle the picture whose name begins with the same sound as **dinosaur**.

What would you do if a dinosaur came to your door?

Name: _____

Beginning Consonant Rr

The <u>r</u>accoon <u>r</u>uns in the <u>r</u>ain.

R r   <u>r</u>accoon

Directions: Say each picture name. Color the space if the picture name begins with the same sound as **raccoon.**

Who does the raccoon visit to get out of the rain?

What does it feel like when you run in the rain?

Beginning Consonant Ff

Where do these <u>f</u>ussy <u>f</u>ireflies land?

F f   <u>f</u>ireflies

Directions: These fussy fireflies only land on things whose names begin with the same sound as **fireflies.** Cut out the pictures at the bottom. Paste them on things in the picture whose names begin with the same sound as **fireflies.**

If a firefly landed on you, what would you do?

Name: _____

Beginning Consonant Gg

What do you see when you wear <u>g</u>oofy <u>g</u>oggles?

G g   <u>goggles</u>

Directions: Say each picture name. If the picture name begins with the same sound as **goggles,** circle it.

What else might you see through these goofy goggles?

Beginning Consonant Mm

<u>M</u>acaroni and <u>m</u>eatballs <u>m</u>ake <u>M</u>ike <u>m</u>essy!

 ## M m   <u>m</u>acaroni <u>m</u>eatballs

Directions: Say each picture name. If the picture name begins with the same sound as **macaroni** and **meatballs,** color the meatball.

What foods make you messy when you eat them?

Name: _____

Review Beginning Consonants

H h

D d

R r

F f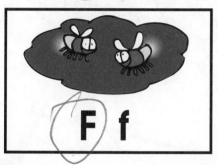

G g

M m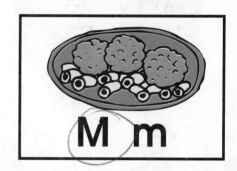

Directions: Look at the letter in each box. Then say each picture name. Circle the picture whose name begins with the sound the letter stands for.

G

D

R

F

M

H

Name: _____

Review Beginning Consonants

Directions: Say each picture name. Listen to the beginning sound. Find the letter that stands for the sound on a crayon. Use your crayons to make each mitten the right color.

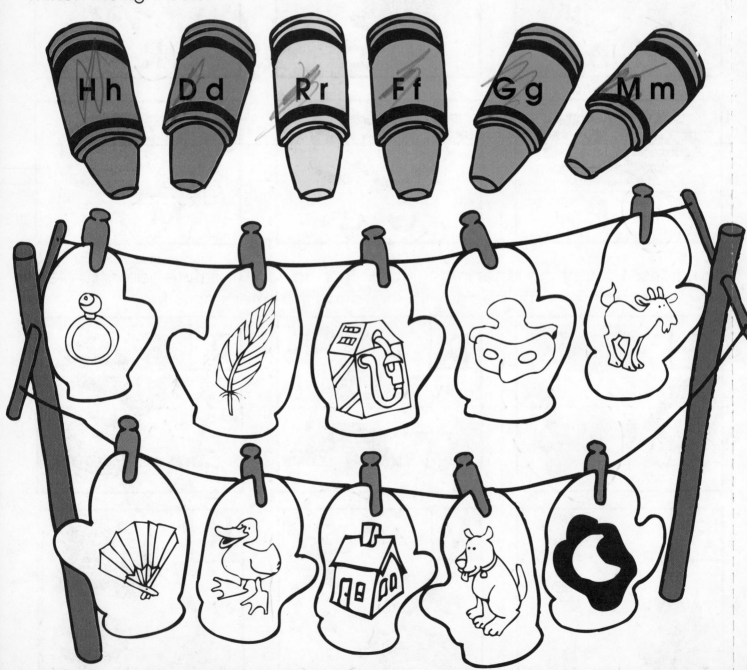

Ending Consonants

 be**d**

bag

 ja**m**

Directions: Write the missing letter to complete each word.

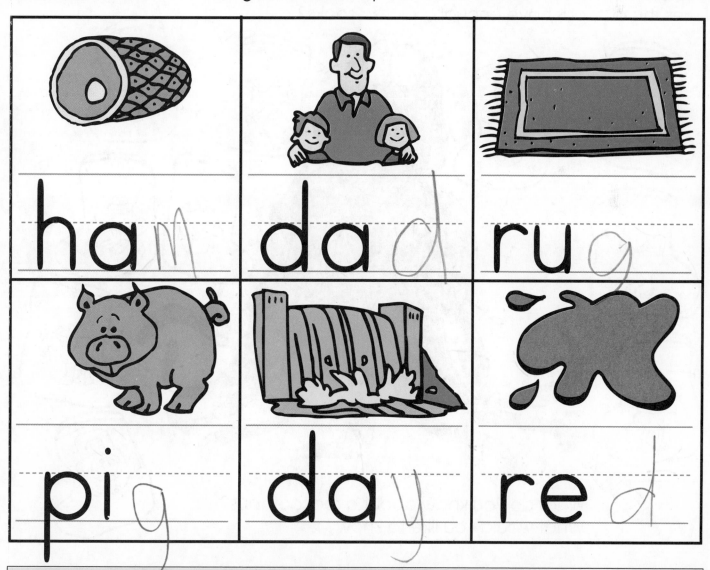

ha m

da d

ru g

pi g

da y

re d

Name: _____

Short Vowel o

This <u>o</u>ctopus wants s<u>o</u>cks.

<u>o</u>ctopus

Directions: Short **o** is the sound you hear at the beginning of the word **octopus.** Say each picture name. Color the sock if you hear the **short o** sound. Does this octopus have enough colored socks?

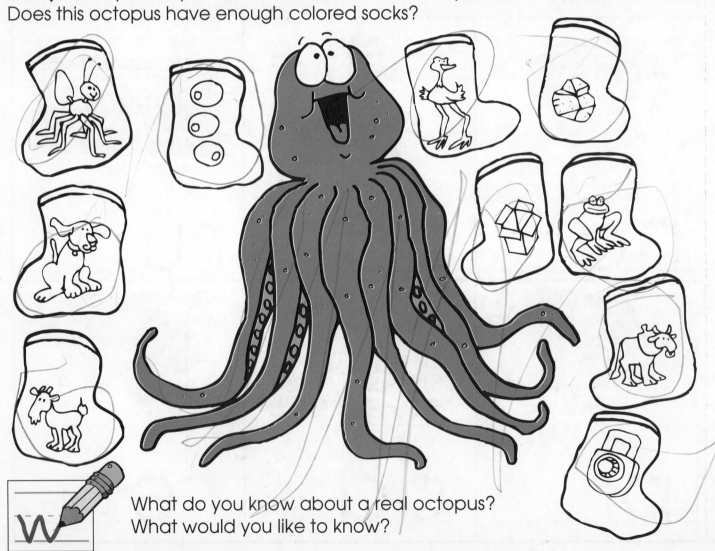

What do you know about a real octopus?
What would you like to know?

Name: _____

Short Vowel o

Directions: Say each picture name. Write **o** if you hear the **short o** sound.

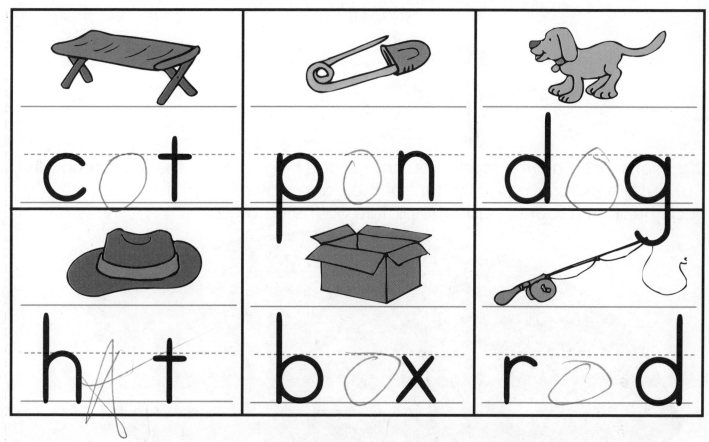

c o t   p o n   d o g

h a t   b o x   r o d

Directions: Use a toy car or pretend your finger is a car at the top of each hill. Smoothly move your finger or car down the hill as you blend the letter sounds to say the name of the picture. Then trace its name on the line.

p o t   m o p

Name: _____

Short Vowel u

Decorate the big beach <u>u</u>mbrella.

<u>u</u>mbrella

Directions: Short **u** is the sound you hear at the beginning of the word **umbrella**. Cut out the pictures at the bottom of the page. Say each picture name. If you hear the **short u** sound, paste the picture on the umbrella.

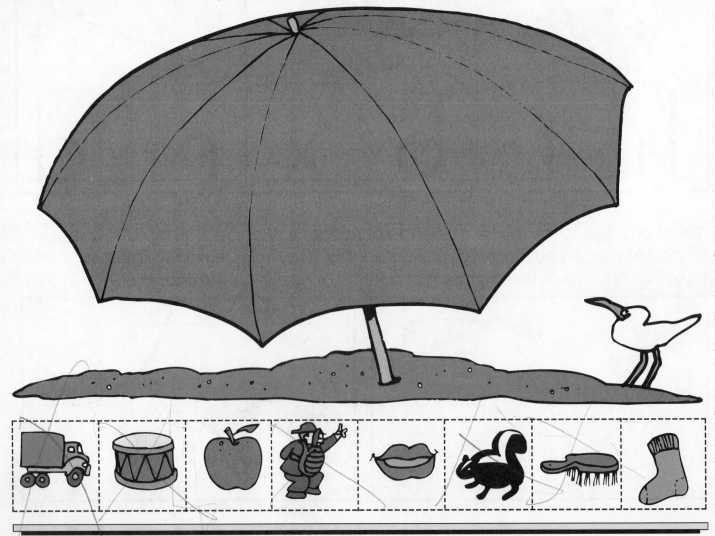

Name: _____

Short Vowel u

Directions: Use a toy car or your finger to smoothly blend the letter sounds to read each word. Then write it on the line.

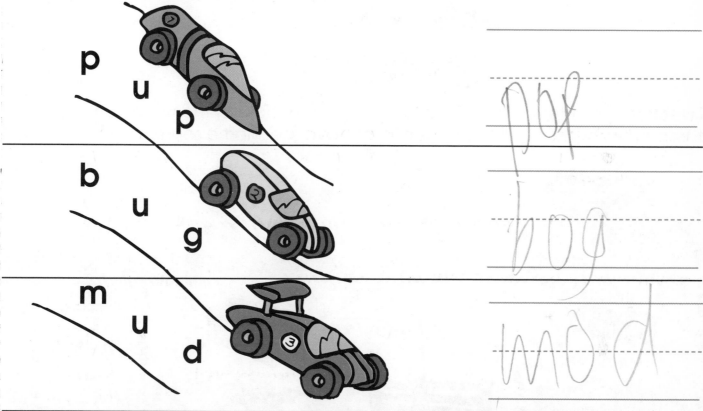

p
u
p

b
u
g

m
u
d

pup

bug

mud

Directions: Write the word from above that names each picture.

mud

bug

mud

What happened the last time you played in the mud?

Name: _____

Short Vowel e

Help the r<u>e</u>d h<u>e</u>n find her <u>e</u>ggs.

 h<u>e</u>n

Directions: Short **e** is the sound you hear in the middle of the word **hen**. Follow the path with the pictures whose names have the short e sound.

What if the red hen lived in a rain forest instead of in a pen on a farm? How would her home be different?

Name: _____

Short Vowel e

Directions: Use a toy car or your finger to smoothly blend the letter sounds to read each word. Write the word on the line. Then write the word that names each picture at the bottom.

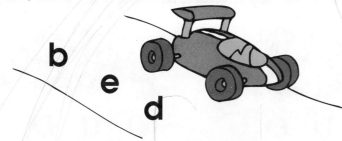

bed

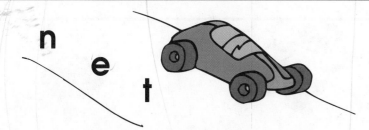

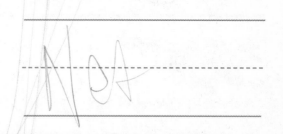

net

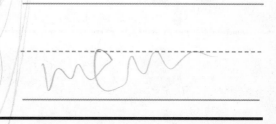

men

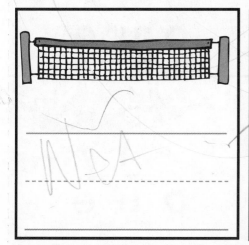

net

men

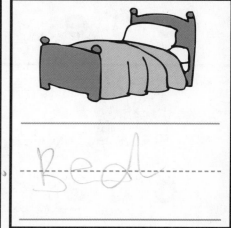

Bed

Review Short Vowels o, u, e

Directions: Say each picture name. Circle the letter that stands for the vowel sound you hear.

Name: _____

Rhyming Words

Directions: Words that have the same ending sounds are called **rhyming words**. Say the names of the pictures. In each row, circle the picture that has the same ending sound as the first picture.

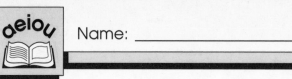

Name: _____

Sound Pattern -at

Pat wears her favorite hat to the costume party.

h**at**

Directions: Cut out the hat and feather. Cut on the dotted lines to make slits. Slip the feather through the hat. Slide the feather and read each new word.

Diagram:

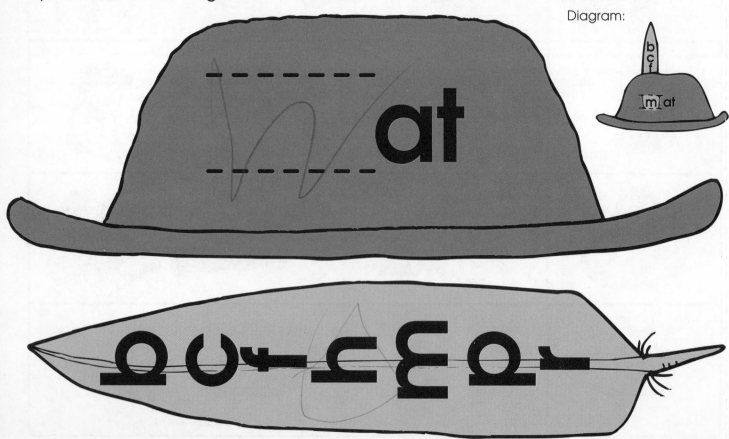

aeiou

Name: _____

Sound Pattern -at

Directions: Name each picture. Think about the beginning sound. Write the letter that belongs at the beginning of each word. The first one is done for you.

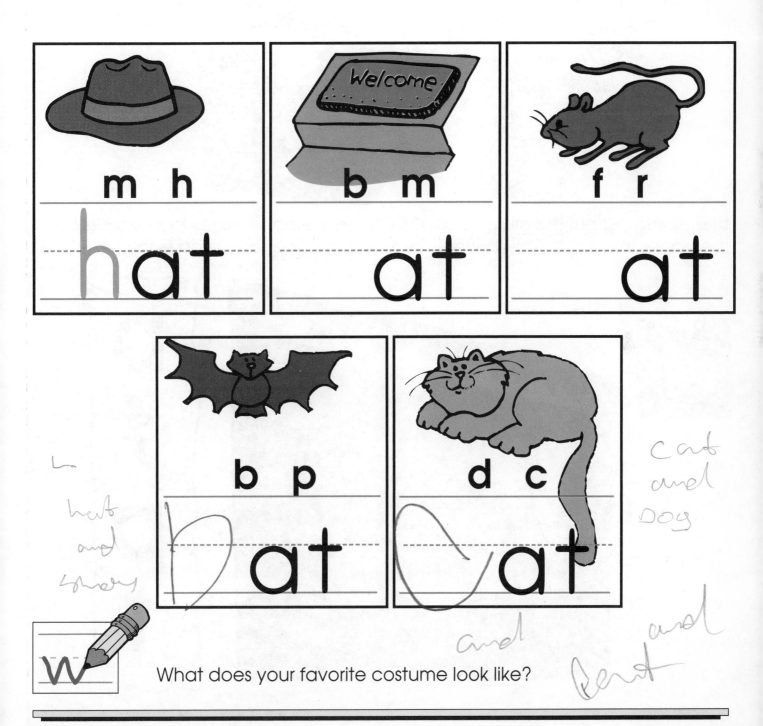

m h

h at

b m

at

f r

at

b p

at

d c

at

cat
and
Dog
and

hat
and
handy

and

W

What does your favorite costume look like?

Sound Pattern -in

Put used paper in the recycling <u>bin</u>. Help save our earth!

b<u>in</u>

Directions: Cut out the bin and paper. Cut on the dotted lines to make slits. Slip the paper through the slits on the bin. Slide the paper and read each new word.

Diagram:

Sound Pattern -in

Directions: Name each picture. Read the words. Circle the word that names the picture. Write it on the line.

fin

tin

_____

_____

_____

pin

bin

_____

_____

_____

pin

fin

_____

_____

_____

tin

pin

_____

_____

_____

What can you do to help save our earth?

Name: _____

Sound Pattern -ot

The <u>tot</u> naps on a <u>cot</u>.

c<u>ot</u>

Directions: You can make a flip book to help you read words. Cut out the cards. Put the big card with the word **cot** on the bottom. Put the letter cards on top of the big card. Staple the cards on the far left side. Then flip the cards and read each word.

Your finished flip book will look like this:

c ot

d g h n p t

Name: _____

Sound Pattern -ot

Directions: Draw a line from each picture to the word that names the picture.

cot

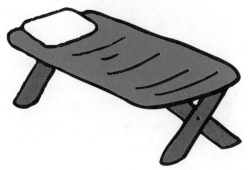

dot

tot

pot

Name: _____

Review Sound Patterns -at, -in, -ot

The <u>tot</u> and the <u>cat</u> reach for the <u>tin</u>.

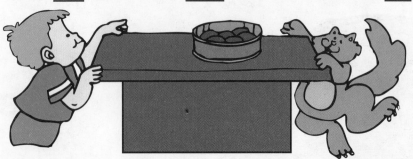

Directions: Name each picture. Cut out the words at the bottom. Paste each word where it belongs.

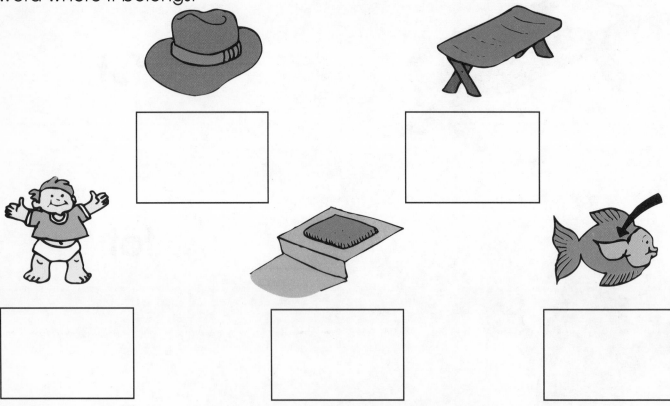

Name: _____

Review Sound Patterns -at, -in, -ot

c<u>at</u>   p<u>ot</u>   b<u>in</u>

Directions: Read each word at the top of the page. Look at the pictures below. Find a rhyming word that belongs with each picture. Write the rhyming word on the line.

pin

_____

- - - - - - - - - - - - - -

_____

hot

_____

- - - - - - - - - - - - - -

_____

fat

_____

- - - - - - - - - - - - - -

_____

Sound Pattern -ug

Can you find the <u>bug</u> in this <u>rug</u>?

b<u>ug</u>

Directions: Cut out the wheels. Put the little wheel on top of the big wheel. Push a straw or a ballpoint pen through the center. Turn the little wheel. How many words can you make?

Your finished word wheel will look like this:

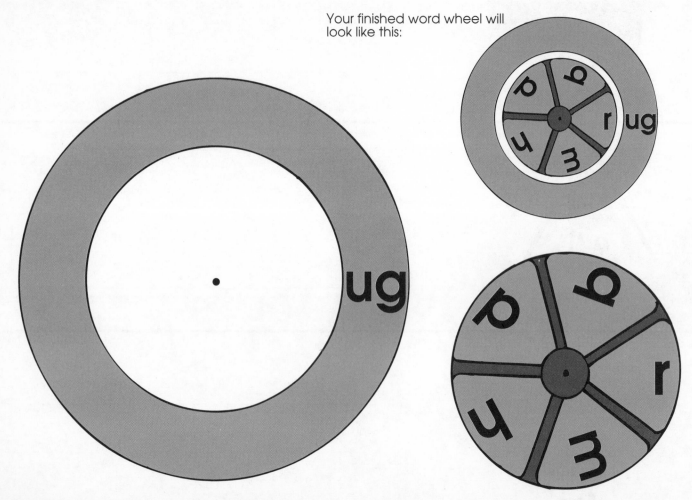

Name: _____

Sound Pattern -ug

Directions: Read each sentence. The pictures will help you. Circle the word that completes the sentence. Then write it on the line.

dug   tug

_____

- -

Pup _____ in the mud.

bug   rug

_____

- -

Pup stops on the _____ .

hug   mug

_____

- -

Mom gives Pup a big _____ .

Name: _____

Sound Pattern -en

K<u>en</u> has t<u>en</u> crayons.

t<u>en</u>

Directions: You can make a flip book to help you read words. Cut out the cards. Put the big card with the word **ten** on the bottom. Put the letter cards on top of the big card. Staple the cards on the far left side. Then flip the cards and read each word.

Your finished flip book will look like this:

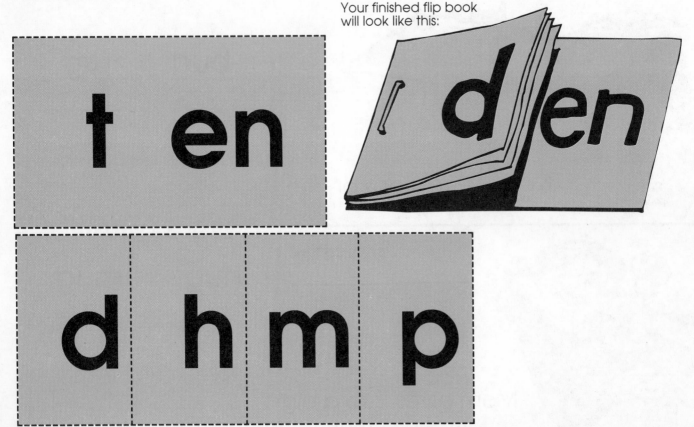

t   en

d   h   m   p

Name: _____

Sound Pattern -en

Directions: Read or ask someone to help you read the rhyme. Circle the word that completes each line. Then write the word on the line.

hen   **den**

_____

"I can't find my eggs!" said the little red _____ .

pen   **men**

_____

She ran by some _____ .

ten   **hen**

_____

She ran by a big _____ .

men   **pen**

_____ !"

"My, what a surprise.
They're right here in my _____ !"

Review Sound Patterns -ug and -en

Directions: Name each picture. Read the question. Circle the word that answers the question. Then write the word.

Is it a **mug** or a **rug**?

_____

Is it **ten** or a **tan**?

_____

Is it a **bug** or a **tug**?

_____

Is it **hen** or a **hug**?

_____

Is it a **pen** or a **cot**?

_____

Name: _____

Review Sound Patterns -at, -in, -ot, -ug, -en

Directions: Read each sentence. The pictures will help you. Circle and write each word that completes the sentence.

hat   bat   rat

_____

- -

Dot hit the ball with her _____ .

---

bug   rug   tug

_____

- -

The friends _____ on the fat rope.

---

pin   tin   bin

_____

- -

Can Ben hit one more _____ ?

---

ten   men   hen

_____

- -

Some _____ dug and dug.

---

pot   dot   cot

_____

- -

Pat put the old tin _____ in the bin.

Name: _____

Review Sound Patterns -at, -in, -ot, -ug, -en

Directions: Read the sentences. Follow the path to help the tot find his cat.

1. Go over the mat.
2. Go under the cot.
3. Go around the pen.
4. Go past a bin.
5. Go around a tug.
6. Take the tot to his cat!

Name: _____

ABC Order

Directions: Draw a line to connect the dots. Follow the letters in ABC order.

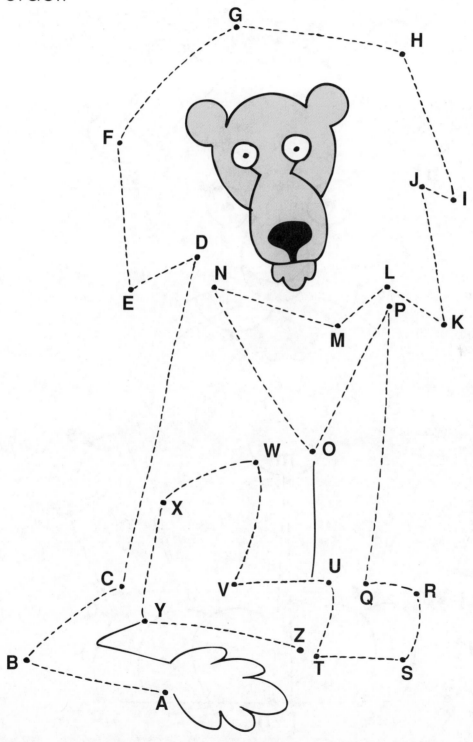

Name: _____

abc Order

Directions: Draw a line to connect the dots. Follow the letters in abc order.

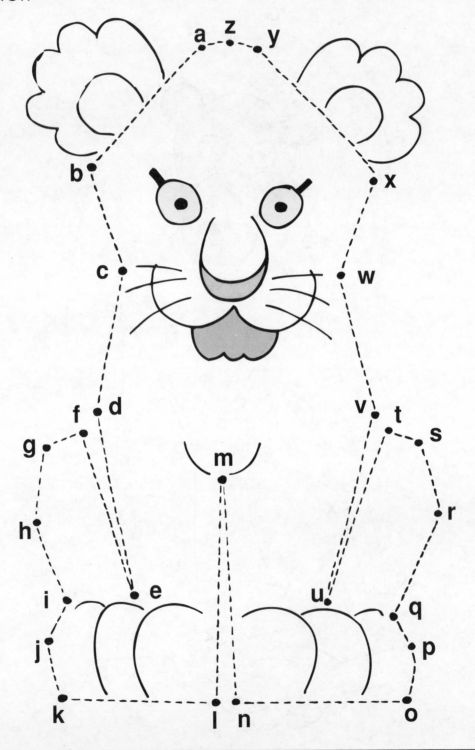

Name: _____

Matching Upper And Lower Case Letters

Directions: Draw a line from each upper case letter to its matching lower case letter.

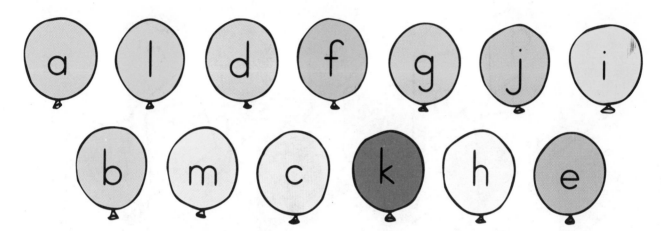

Matching Upper And Lower Case Letters

Directions: Draw a line from each upper case letter to its matching lower case letters.

Name: _____

Discrimination Of a, b, d

Directions: Color the butterflies.
a = yellow, b = orange, d = purple

Name: _____

Writing Upper Case Letters

Directions: Trace each letter. Write each letter again next to the letter you traced.

Name: _____

Writing Lower Case Letters

Directions: Trace each letter. Write each letter again next to the letter you traced.

Name: _____

Review

Directions: Fill in the missing upper and lower case letters to complete the alphabet.

Name: _____

Beginning Consonant Sounds Bb, Cc, Dd

Directions: Say the sound that the letters Bb, Cc, Dd make. (Bb = buh, Cc = kuh, Dd = duh). Then say the name of each picture. If the first sound matches the letter, color it blue.

Beginning Consonant Sounds Ff, Gg, Hh

Directions: Say the sounds for the letters Ff, Gg, Hh. (Ff = fuh, Gg = guh, Hh = huh). Draw a circle around the picture if it begins with the letter in the column.

Name: _____

Beginning Sounds Jj, Kk, Ll

Directions: Draw a line from each picture to its beginning letter sound.

Jj

Kk

Ll

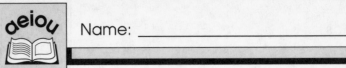

Beginning Consonant Sounds Mm, Nn, Pp

Directions: Say the sound the letters Mm, Nn, and Pp make.
(Mm = muh, Nn = nuh, Pp = puh). Color the picture if its
beginning sound matches the letter.

Name: _____

Beginning Consonant Sounds Qq, Rr, Ss

Directions: Say the sound that the letters Qq, Rr, Ss make. (Qq = quh, Rr = ruh, Ss = sss.) Draw a line from each picture to its matching letter.

Qq

Rr

Ss

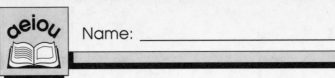

Name: _____

Beginning Consonant Sounds Tt, Vv, Ww

Directions: Say the sound that the letters Tt, Vv, Ww make. (T t= tuh, Vv = vuh, Ww = wuh.) Color each picture if it has the same beginning sound as the letter.

Beginning Consonant Sounds Xx, Yy, Zz

Directions: Say the sound that the letters Xx, Yy, Zz make. (Xx = zuh, as in xylophone; Yy = yuh; Zz = zuh. Sometimes Xx says its own name, as in xray.) Draw a circle around each picture if its beginning sound matches the letter.

Name: _____

Review

Directions: Look at each picture. Say its name. Write the lower case letter for the beginning sound in each picture.

Name: _____

Beginning Short Vowel Sounds: A

Directions: Say the sound for the letter Aa. (The short vowel sound for Aa is heard at the beginning of the word alligator.) Color the pictures that begin with the short vowel sound.

Beginning Short Vowel Sounds: Ee

Directions: Say the short vowel sound for the letter Ee. (It makes the same sound as the "e" in the word egg.) Look at the pictures. Color the pictures if they begin with the sound of the short vowel Ee.

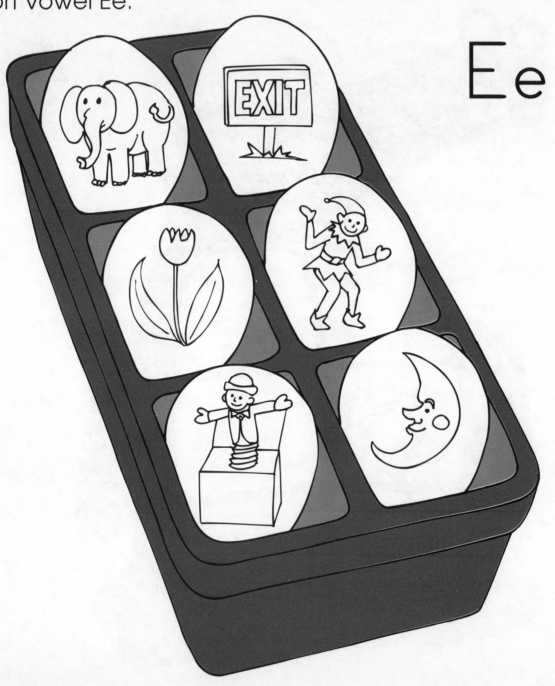

Name: _____

Beginning Short Vowel Sounds: Ii

Directions: Say the short vowel sound for the letter Ii. (The short vowel sound for the letter Ii sounds like the "I" in Indian.) Look at the pictures. Color the pictures that begin with the short vowel sound of Ii.

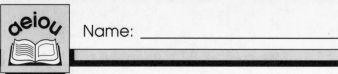

Name: _____

Beginning Short Vowel Sounds: Oo

Directions: Say the short vowel sound for Oo. (It makes the same sound as the "O" in Oscar.) Look at the pictures. Color the pictures that begin with the sound of Oo.

Name: _____

Beginning Short Vowel Sounds: Uu

Directions: 1) Say the sound for the letter Uu. (It makes the same sound as the "u" in umbrella.) 2) Look at the pictures and say each word. 3) Draw pictures of your uncle, something that goes up and an umbrella.

uncle

up

umbrella

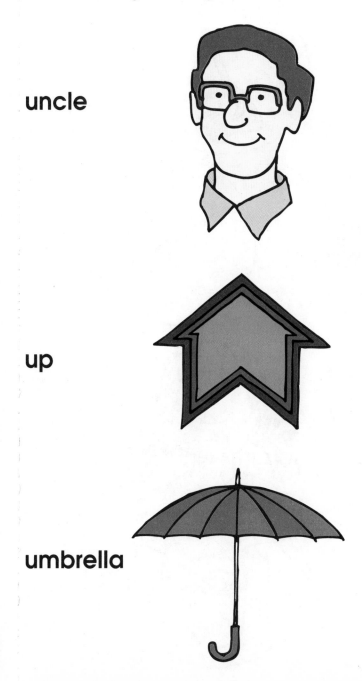

Middle Sounds With Short Vowels

Directions: Say the name of each picture. Listen for the middle sound. Draw a line between the picture and its matching letter.

Name: _____

Middle Sounds: Short Vowel Sounds

Directions: Look at the pictures. Write the letter for the sound you hear in the middle of the word.

Name: _____

Review

Directions: 1) Look at each picture and say its name. 2) Write the beginning or middle vowel sound that you hear. 3) If you hear the sound at the beginning of the word, color the picture blue. 4) If you hear the sound in the middle of the word, color the picture yellow.

Name: _____

Words With Short Vowel Aa

Directions: Read the words. Draw a line from the picture to its matching word.

Name: _____

Words With Short Vowel Ee

Directions: Read the words. Circle the picture whose sound has short vowel e.

net

fence

bell

ten

Name: _____

Words With Short Vowel Ii

Directions: Read the words. Draw a line from each word to its matching picture.

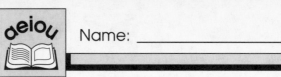

Name: _____

Words With Short Vowel Oo

Directions: Look at the pictures and read the words. Draw a line from each picture to the word that describes it.

aeiou

Name: _____

Words With Short Vowel Uu

Directions: Look at the pictures and read the words. Draw a line between each picture and the word that describes it.

bus

cup

gum

bug

Name: _____

Review

Directions: Look at the pictures and read the words. Draw a line between each picture and the word that describes it.

pig

duck

cat

fox

map

fish

net

bus

top

bed

Name: _____

Which Are Opposites?

Directions: Draw a line between the opposites.

boy

under

over

sad

in

girl

happy

out

Name: _____

What Belongs?

Directions: Color the pictures in each row that belong together. Draw an **X** through the one that does not belong.

| snowman | sled | skates | ball |

| dog | jar | rabbit | cat |

| book | shoe | sock | boot |

| helicopter | plane | tree | balloon |

Name: _____

What Comes Before?

Directions: Draw a circle around the small picture that shows what happened right before the pictures in the big boxes.

What Comes After?

Directions: Look at the large pictures. Draw a circle around the small picture that shows what would happen next.

Name: _____

Story Order

Directions: Find the four pictures that tell a story. Color them.
Write numbers in the boxes to show the order they belong in.

Name: _____

Story Sense

Directions: Look at the large pictures. Draw a circle around the small box that shows what is more likely to happen next.

Name: _____

Review

Directions: Draw lines to match the opposites.

big   hot   open   up

cold   down   little   closed

Directions: Cross out the picture that doesn't belong.

Directions: Circle the picture that shows what comes before.

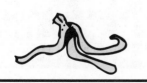      

Name: _____

Review

Directions: Circle the picture that shows what comes after.

Directions: Write numbers in the boxes to show what order they belong in.

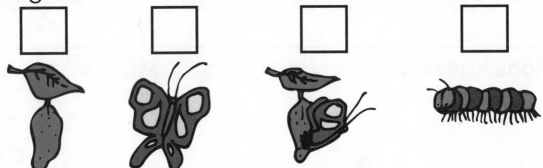

Directions: Circle the picture that shows what is likely to happen next.

Name: _____

Rhyming Pairs

Directions: Circle the pairs that rhyme.
(Words with the same ending sounds.)

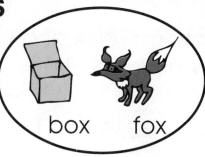

box   fox

map   nest

dog   frog

cake   cap

hat   bat

kite   mop

star   jar

can   fan

rat   pig

dish   fish

book   bottle

sock   clock

sun   leaf

nose   hose

beet   feet

ball   bird

Name: _____

Rhyming Game

Directions: Think of a word that rhymes with the word given. Draw a picture. Write the word.

cat

_____

_____

_____

pan

_____

_____

_____

bug

_____

_____

_____

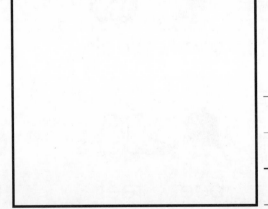

Name: _____

Beginning Sounds

Directions: Look at the picture in each box. Say its name. Color the pictures in that row beginning with the same sound.

Name: _____

Words That Start With L

Directions: Color the picture in each box that starts like **lamb**.

Name: _____

More Beginning Sounds

Directions: Look at the pictures. Say their names. Draw a line between pictures beginning with the same sound.

bee

door

pillow

turtle

drum

bug

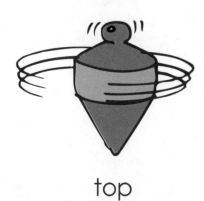

top

pig

Name: _____

Words That Begin With r

Directions: Color the picture. Circle the six things that start with the sound of the letter **r**.

Name: _____

Beginning Sounds

Directions: Look at each picture. Say its name. Circle the letter the word begins with.

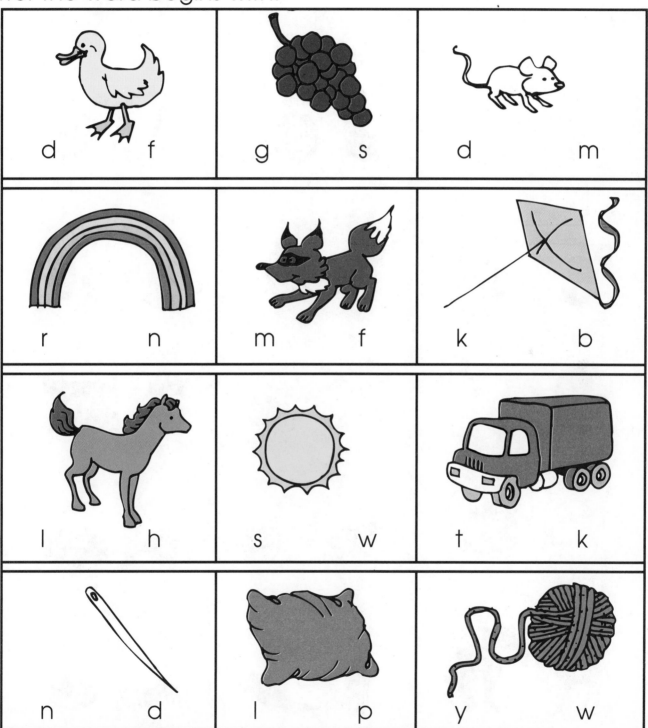

d f	g s	d m
r n	m f	k b
l h	s w	t k
n d	l p	y w

Review

Directions: Circle the pairs that start with the same letter.

Name: _____

Words With a

Directions: Write the letter **a** to finish each word. Draw a line to match the word and its picture.

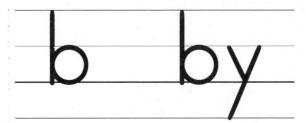

b__by

c__t

m__p

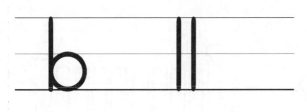

b__ll

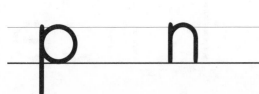

p__n

Name: _____

Words With e

Directions: Color the pictures. Say the name of each picture. Write the letter **e** to finish each word.

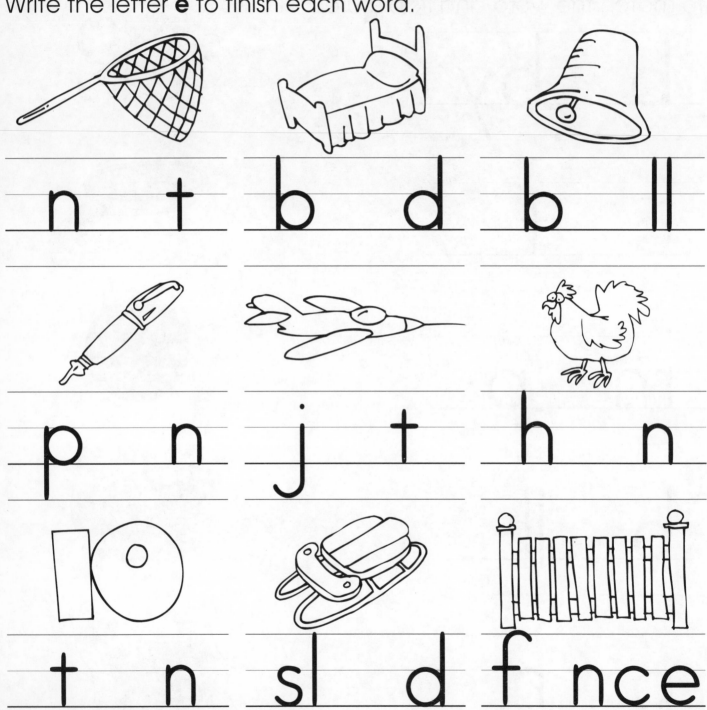

n __ t   b __ d   b __ ll

p __ n   j __ t   h __ n

t __ n   sl __ d   f __ nce

Name: _____

Words With i

Directions: Say the name of each picture. Draw lines from the dish to the pictures with the same middle sound.

Directions: Write the letter **i** to finish each word. Say the words.

f___sh   p___g   p___n

Name: _____

Words With o

Directions: Write the letter **o** to finish each word. Say the word.

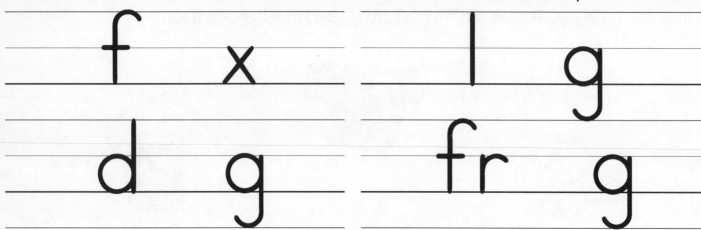

f x

l g

d g

fr g

Directions: Find the pictures of the words you just wrote and circle them.

Name: _____

Words With u

Directions: Write the letter **u** to finish each word. Say the word. Draw a line to match each word with its picture.

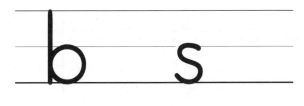

Phonics

Name: _____

Middle Sounds

Directions: Look at the picture in each box. Say its name. Color the pictures in that row that have the same middle sound.

106

Name: _____

Middle Sounds

Directions: Look at the picture. Say its name. Draw a line to the letter that makes its middle sound.

a

e

i

o

u

Name: _____

Review

Directions: Trace the letters.

Directions: Say the name of each picture. Write the correct letter to finish each word.

b   l l   p   g   c   p

b   d   d   g   p   n

Name: _____

Ending Sounds

Directions: Look at the picture in each box. Say its name.
Color the pictures in each row that end with the same sound.

Name: _____

Ending Sounds

Directions: Look at the picture in each box. Say its name.
Circle the letter that the word ends with.

Name: _____

Word Families

Directions: Say the name of the picture in the box. Color the pictures in each row that have the same ending sound.

Words That End With an

Directions: Say the name of each picture. Draw a line to match each picture with its word.
Write the missing letter.

f n

c n

p n

Directions: Can you write the word that matches this picture?

_____

_____

Name: _____

Words That End With at

Directions: Say the name of the picture. Write the missing letters.

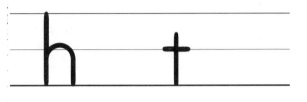

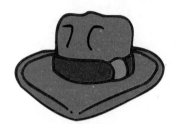

h ___ t

Directions: Write these words that end the same as hat.

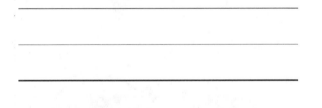

Directions: Can you think of another word that sounds like hat? Write the word. Draw the picture.

Name: _____

Review

Directions: Trace the words.

fat   red   big

Directions: Look at each picture. Say the word. Pick a word from the top with the same ending as the word in the picture. Write the words to finish the sentences.

The bed is red.

The _____ is _____.

The _____ is _____.

Name: _____

Beginning Consonant Ff

<u>F</u>ind the number on the <u>f</u>irefighter's truck.

F f <u>f</u>irefighter

Directions: Say each picture name. If the picture name begins with the same sound as **firefighter**, color the space.

Would you like to be a firefighter? Why or why not?

Name: _____

Beginning Consonant Mm

How <u>m</u>any <u>m</u>onkeys <u>m</u>eet at the <u>m</u>ovie?

M m <u>m</u>onkeys

Directions: Cut out the pictures at the bottom. Paste them beside things in the picture whose names begin with the same sound as **monkeys**.

Will the monkeys misbehave at the movie?
What kind of mischief might they make?

Beginning Consonant Ss

On <u>s</u>unny days, <u>S</u>umi plays in her <u>s</u>andbox.

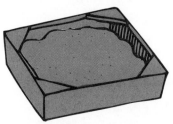

S s   <u>s</u>andbox

Directions: Sumi only plays with things that begin with the same sound as **sandbox.** Say the picture names. Draw a line from Sumi to each picture whose name begins with the same sound as **sandbox.**

What do you like to do on sunny days?

Name: _____

Beginning Consonant Ll

Help the little lost lamb find its mother.

L l   lamb

Directions: Cut out the picture of the lamb at the bottom. Use the picture to follow the path to its mother. Each time you pass a picture whose name begins with the same sound as **lamb**, mark an **l** on it. When you are through, paste the baby next to its mother.

A lamb's parents are called sheep. List the names of other animal babies and their parents.

Name: _____

Beginning Consonant Nn

Can you make a <u>n</u>ecklace out of <u>n</u>uts?

N n   <u>n</u>ecklace

Directions: Say the picture name on each nut on the necklace. If the picture name begins with the same sound as **necklace**, color the nut.

Explain how to make something using things found in nature. Be sure the steps are in the right order.

Name: _____

Beginning Consonant Vv

Look out! The <u>v</u>olcano is ready to erupt!

V v   <u>v</u>olcano

Directions: Cut out the pictures at the bottom. Say each picture name. If the picture name begins with the same sound as **volcano**, paste it on the volcano.

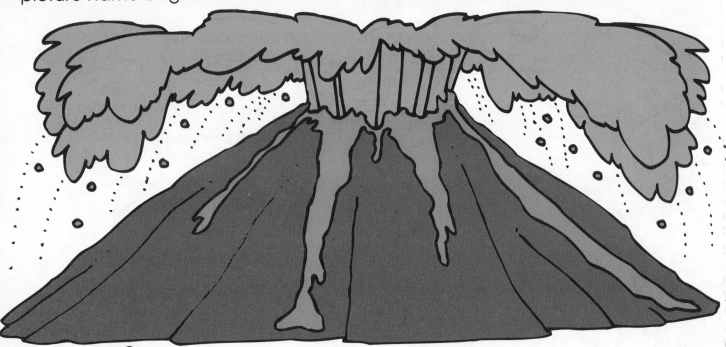

What do you know about volcanoes?
What would you like to find out about volcanoes?

Name: _____

Beginning Consonant Bb

You can keep <u>b</u>uns in a <u>b</u>asket.

B b   <u>b</u>asket

Directions: Look at the pictures that show how baskets can be used. Say each picture name. If the picture name begins with the same sound as **buns** and **basket**, color it.

Think of other ways to use baskets.
Your ideas can be silly or sensible.

Name: _____

Beginning Consonant Cc

<u>C</u>arla is looking for a team <u>c</u>ap.

C c <u>c</u>ap

Directions: Cut out the pictures at the bottom. Say each picture name. If the picture name begins with the same sound as **cap**, paste it on a cap.

If you could meet your favorite team player, what would you ask him or her?

Name: _____

Beginning Consonant Pp

Come to <u>P</u>ete's <u>p</u>izza <u>p</u>arty!

P p   <u>p</u>izza

Directions: Pete is so picky he only serves foods whose names begin with the same sound as **pizza** at his party. What else does Pete serve? Say the picture names. Draw a line from Pete to each picture whose name begins with the same sound as **pizza**.

What foods would you serve at a party? Plan a menu.
Ask if you can use the menu for your next birthday party.

Name: _____

Beginning Consonant Tt

<u>T</u>une in <u>t</u>o your favorite <u>t</u>elevision show.

T t <u>t</u>elevision

Directions: Cut out the pictures at the bottom. Say each picture name. If the picture name begins with the same sound as **television**, paste it on the television.

What do you think of this?
Children should only watch television one hour a week.

Name: _____

Beginning Consonant Gg

What gift did the girl get?

G g gift

Directions: Say each picture name. Color the space if the picture name begins with the same sound as **gift**.

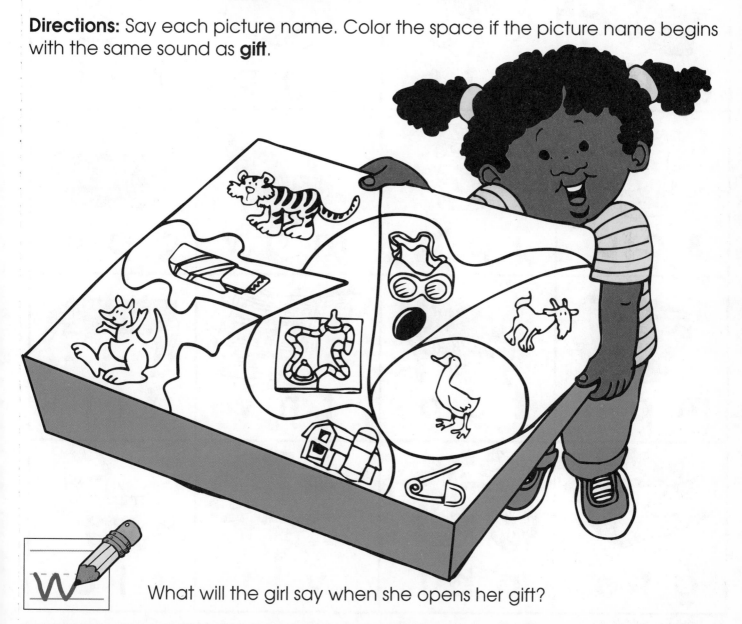

What will the girl say when she opens her gift?

Reviewing Beginning Consonants

Directions: Say each picture name. Circle the letter that stands for the beginning sound.

p m n	v t s	f g p	b t l
s c p	l p b	m g v	g p n
m p n	t g p	f n v	f l t
g f c	p b f	v l t	s l c

Name: _____

Short Vowel a

How many people c<u>a</u>n fit in a v<u>a</u>n?

v<u>a</u>n

Directions: Short **a** is the sound you hear in the middle of the word **van**. Pretend your finger is a van at the top of the hill. Smoothly move your finger down the hill as you blend the letter sounds to read each word. Then write the word on the line.

g
a
s
_____
- - - - - - - - - - - - - - - -
_____

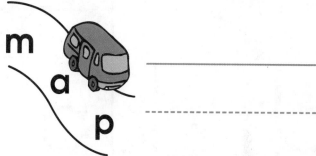

m
a
p
_____
- - - - - - - - - - - - - - - -
_____

Directions: Write the word from above that names each picture.

_____
- - - - - - - - - - - - - -
_____

- - - - - - - - - - - - - -
_____

Name: _____

Short Vowel i

This p<u>i</u>g likes to d<u>i</u>g and d<u>i</u>g.

p<u>i</u>g

Directions: Short **i** is the sound you hear in the middle of the word **pig**. Say each picture name. Write **i** if you hear the short **i** sound.

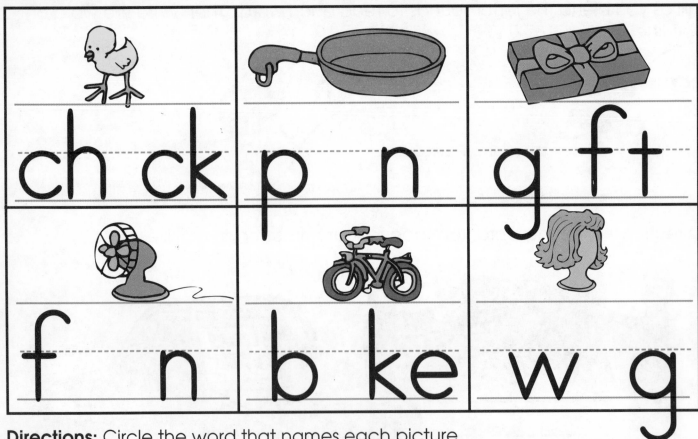

ch ck   p n   g ft

f n   b ke   w g

Directions: Circle the word that names each picture.

 **big fit bib**

 pan pig pin

Name: _____

Beginning Consonant Rr

Welcome to the <u>r</u>emarkable animal <u>r</u>anch.
Look! There's a <u>r</u>abbit <u>r</u>acing on <u>r</u>oller skates!

R r <u>r</u>abbit

Directions: Say the picture name of each remarkable animal. If the picture
name begins like **rabbit**, mark an **r** it.

Write a comic strip about the remarkable animal ranch.

Name: _____

Beginning Consonant Kk

Look at the <u>k</u>ites in the big tree!

K k <u>k</u>ite

Directions: Cut out the pictures at the bottom. Say each picture name. If the picture name begins with the same sound as **kite,** paste it on a kite in the tree.

If your kite were up high in a tree, how would you get it down?

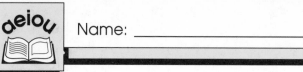 Name: _____

Beginning Consonant Jj

<u>J</u>ack put too much <u>j</u>unk in his <u>j</u>eep.

J j   <u>j</u>eep

Directions: Say the picture name for each piece of junk in Jack's jeep. If the picture name begins with the same sound as **jeep**, mark a **j** on it.

Finish this sentence: I have too much junk in my _____ , but

_____ .

Beginning Consonant Ww

Winnie Walrus wants to play in the waves.

W w   walrus

Directions: Help Winnie get to the ocean water. Follow the path with the pictures whose names begin with the same sound as **walrus**.

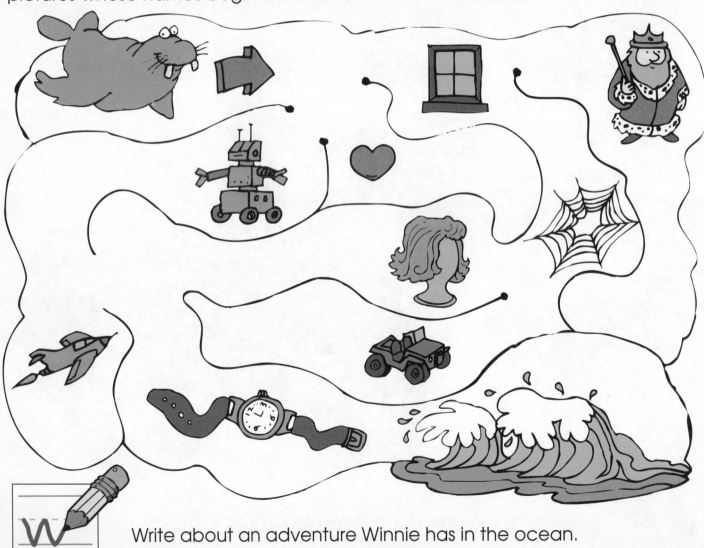

Write about an adventure Winnie has in the ocean.

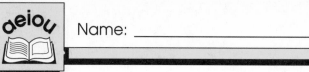

Name: _____

Beginning Consonant Hh

Who is <u>h</u>iding in the farmer's <u>h</u>ay?

 **H h**   **<u>h</u>ay**

Directions: Say each picture name. Color the space if the picture name begins with the same sound as **hay**.

Imagine you are a farmer. What is your farm like?
What do you do for fun?

Beginning Consonant Dd

<u>D</u>oughnut ice cream is my favorite <u>d</u>essert!

D d   <u>d</u>oughnuts

Directions: Cut out the pictures at the bottom. Say each picture name. If the picture name begins with the same sound as **doughnuts,** paste it on the dish of doughnut ice cream.

Invent a new kind of dessert.
Draw a picture to go with your writing.

Name: _____

Beginning Consonant Yy

<u>Y</u>uriko knits a <u>y</u>arn blanket for her great grandson.

Y y   <u>y</u>arn

Directions: Say the picture names in each square on Yuriko's blanket. Circle the picture whose name begins with the same sound as **yarn**.

Write about something special that someone made for you.

Name: _____

Beginning Sounds Qu/qu

How <u>qu</u>ickly can you decorate the <u>qu</u>een's crown?

Qu qu <u>qu</u>een

Directions: Cut out the pictures at the bottom. Say each picture name. If the picture name begins with the same sounds as **queen**, paste it on her crown.

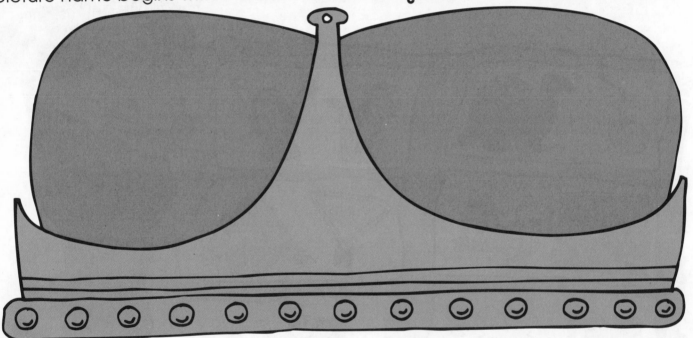

If you could be <u>qu</u>een or king of the world for a day, what would you do?

Name: _____

Beginning Consonant Zz

Step inside the <u>z</u>any <u>z</u>oo!

Z z   <u>Z</u>OO

Directions: Circle three zany pictures whose names begin with the same sound as **zoo**.

TICKETS 0¢

What else might you see in a zany zoo?

Name: _____

Ending Consonant x

Rex is si**x** today.

 **X x   six**

Directions: The word **six ends** with the sounds that the letter **x** stands for. Help Rex get to his birthday cake. Follow the path with the pictures whose names **end** with the same sounds as **six**.

What do you think of this? Six is the best age of all!

Name: _____

Reviewing Beginning Consonants

Directions: Look at the letters in the boxes. Then say each picture name. Draw a line from the letter to the picture whose name begins with the sound that the letter stands for.

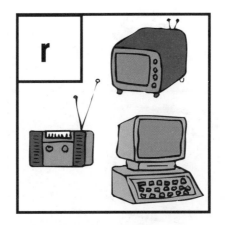

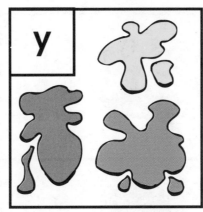

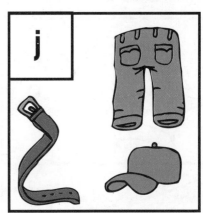

Name: _____

Ending Consonants

Directions: Say each picture name. Fill in the circle next to the letter that stands for the last sound.

Example:
- ● p
- ○ d
- ○ m

○ l ○ d ○ t	○ x ○ v ○ d	○ f ○ x ○ n
○ l ○ b ○ n	○ m ○ f ○ s	○ g ○ f ○ x
○ s ○ v ○ m	○ x ○ m ○ t	○ n ○ p ○ b
○ s ○ p ○ f	○ n ○ d ○ b	○ g ○ t ○ b

Consonant Blends

The <u>fr</u>og <u>st</u>opped on the <u>pl</u>ant.

Directions: The sounds you hear at the beginning of **frog**, **stopped**, and **plant** are consonant blends. Say the name of the first picture in each row. Circle each picture in the row whose name begins with the same blend.

Name: _____

Short Vowel o

The f<u>o</u>x h<u>o</u>ps over the l<u>o</u>g.

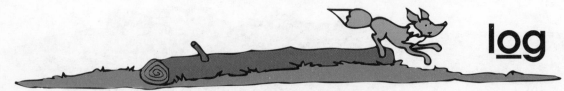

l<u>o</u>g

Directions: Short **o** is the sound you hear in the middle of the word **log**. Look at the picture. Read the sentence and circle the word that completes it. Then write the word on the line.

Don and Todd sit on the _____.		cot cat got
Tom got a tan _____.		dig dog jog
A top is in the big _____.		fox box fog
Mom has the hot _____.		pot pat pop
Dot's job is to _____.		mat mop mob

Name: _____

Short Vowel u

Would you like to h<u>u</u>g the p<u>u</u>p?

p<u>u</u>p

Directions: Short **u** is the sound you hear in the middle of the word **pup**. Underline the sentence that tells about each picture.

The gum is on the rug.

The pup jumps in the tub.

Bud will run to the bus.

The cub is in the sun.

Name: _____

Short Vowel e

The little spider left its w<u>e</u>b.

w<u>e</u>b

Directions: Short **e** is the sound you hear in the middle of the word **web**. Circle the word that will complete each sentence. Read the sentence again to be sure that it makes sense. Then write the word on the line.

1. Peg will get in _____.   **bed   web   hen**

2. Ed fed his _____.   **peg   pot   pet**

3. A red hen is in a _____.   **pen   peg   pep**

4. Bev has a wet _____.   **let   leg   led**

5. The ten men get on the _____. **jet   met   bet**

6. Chet sat on the top _____.   **pep   stop   step**

7. Get the bug in the _____.   **not   net   nut**

Name: _____

Sound Pattern -an

Can you make a fan?

f**an**

Directions: Say each picture name. Circle the word that names the picture. Write the word on the line.

can	_____	can	_____
fan	-------	tan	-------
ran	_____	pan	_____

pan	_____	man	_____
ran	-------	ran	-------
man	_____	van	_____

Directions: Draw a picture to go with this sentence.

Dan has a tan van.

Sound Pattern -it

Kit will <u>sit</u> and read a little flip book.

s<u>it</u>

Directions: You can make a little flip book to help you read words. Cut out the cards. Put the big card with the word **sit** on the bottom. Put the letter cards on top of the big card. Staple the cards on the far left side. Then flip the cards and read each word.

Your finished flip book
will look like this:

s it

b it

b   f   h   p   qu

Name: _____

Sound Pattern -og

Early in the morning, Bob feeds the h<u>og</u>.

h<u>og</u>

Directions: Read the rhyme to find out what Bob does next. Circle the word that completes each sentence. Then write the word on the line.

Every day Bob likes to _____ .

jog
dog
fog

Can he see in all this _____ ?

hog
frog
fog

Bob trips on a fat _____ .

No, Bob trips on a fat _____ .

dog
log
jog

But he gets help from his big _____ !

hog
fog
dog

Name: _____

Sound Pattern -ub

The <u>sub</u> is going under!

s<u>ub</u>

Directions: Cut out the sub and the scope. Cut on the dotted lines to make slits. Slip the scope through the slits on the sub. Slide the scope and read each new word.

Diagram:

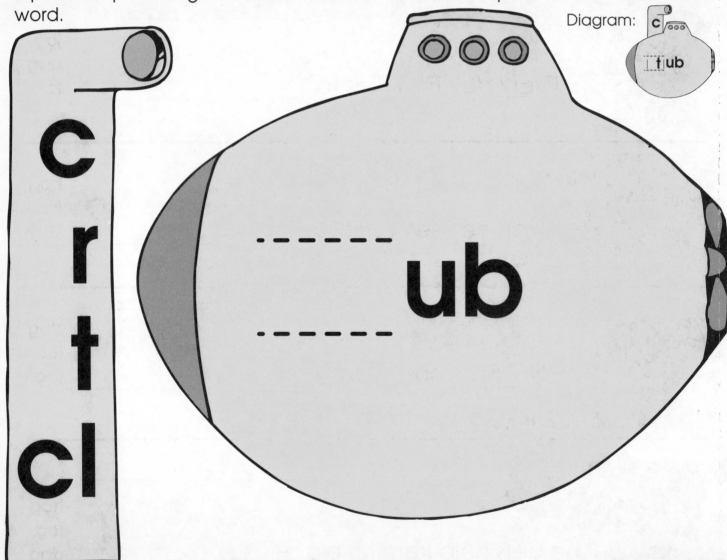

Name: _____

Sound Pattern -et

Will you **let** me?

No, not **yet**!

l**et**

Directions: Look at the pictures. Read each sentence. Match the sentences with the pictures by drawing a line.

I want to hit the net!

I want a big, big pet!

I want to get real wet!

I want to fly a jet!

Name: _____

Long Vowel a

Can you p<u>lay</u> the tr<u>ai</u>n g<u>ame</u> on this tr<u>ay</u>?

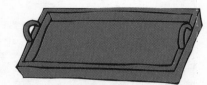

tr<u>ai</u>n   g<u>a</u>m<u>e</u>   tr<u>ay</u>

Directions: Long **a** is the sound you hear in the words **train**, **game**, and **tray**. Say each picture name on the game. Circle the picture if you hear the long **a** sound.

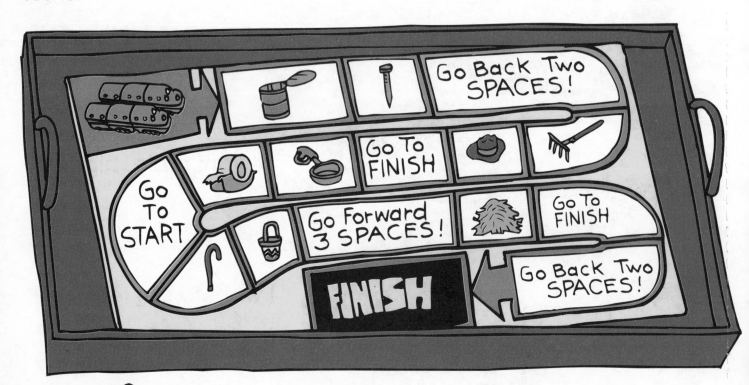

Write rules for this train game.
Use your rules to play the game with a friend.

Name: _____

Long Vowel a

Directions: Say the name of each picture. Circle the letters that stand for the long **a** sound in the picture name. The first ones show you what to do.

v(a)s(e)

s(a)i l

p(a)y

m a i l

j a y

c a p e

l a k e

s a f e

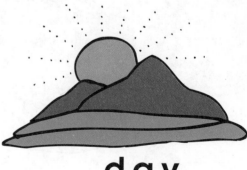

d a y

Name: _____

Long Vowel i

M<u>i</u>k<u>e</u> will d<u>i</u>v<u>e</u> for a d<u>i</u>m<u>e</u>.

 d<u>i</u>m<u>e</u>

Directions: Long **i** is the sound you hear in the word **dime**. Mike only dives for things whose names have the long **i** sound.
Circle the things Mike will dive for.

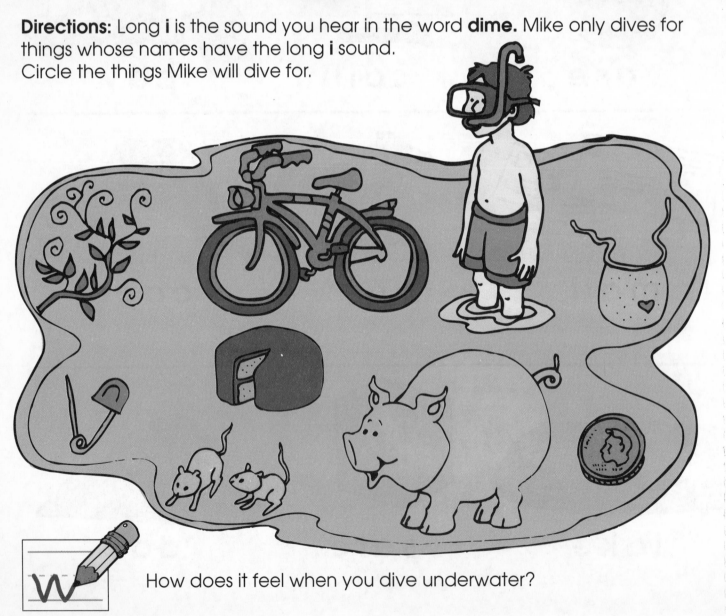

How does it feel when you dive underwater?

Long Vowel i

Directions: Words that have the same ending sounds are called rhyming words. Read the words on each kite. Color the kites that have three rhyming long **i** words.

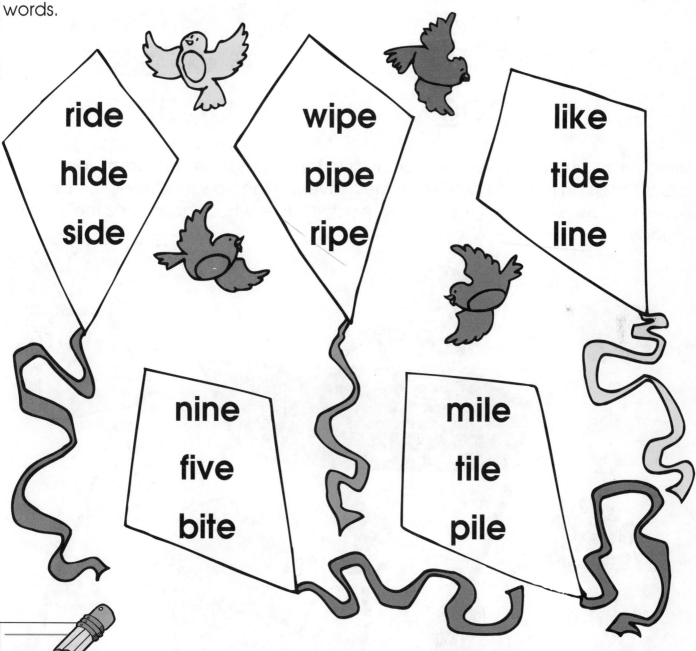

ride
hide
side

wipe
pipe
ripe

like
tide
line

nine
five
bite

mile
tile
pile

Write a short rhyme using the words on one of the kites you colored.

Long Vowel o

Joan loads a rope on her boat.

rope

boat

Directions: Long **o** is the sound you hear in the words **rope** and **boat**. Joan only loads things on her boat whose names have the long **o** sound. Say the picture names. Draw a line from the boat to each picture whose name has the long **o** sound.

Name: _____

Long Vowel o

Directions: Say the name of each picture. Finish the name by writing **o** and **e** or **oa** when you hear the long **o** sound.

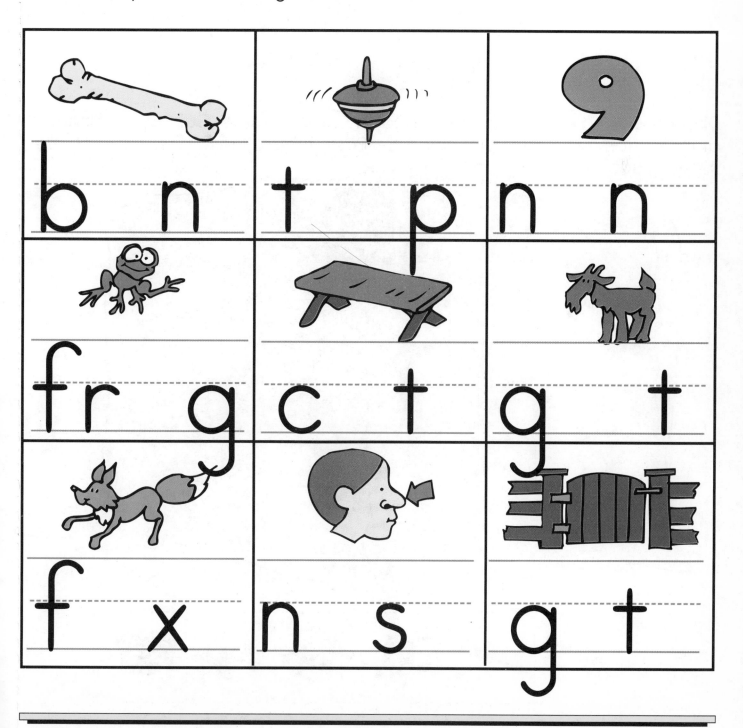

b _ n   t _ p _ n   n _ n

f r _ g   c _ t   g _ t

f _ x   n _ s   g _ t

Name: _____

Long Vowel u

The c<u>u</u>te cub sits on a c<u>u</u>b<u>e</u>.

c<u>u</u>b<u>e</u>

Directions: Long **u** is the sound you hear in the word **cube.** Cut out the pictures at the bottom. Say each picture name. Paste the pictures whose names have the long **u** sound on the cube.

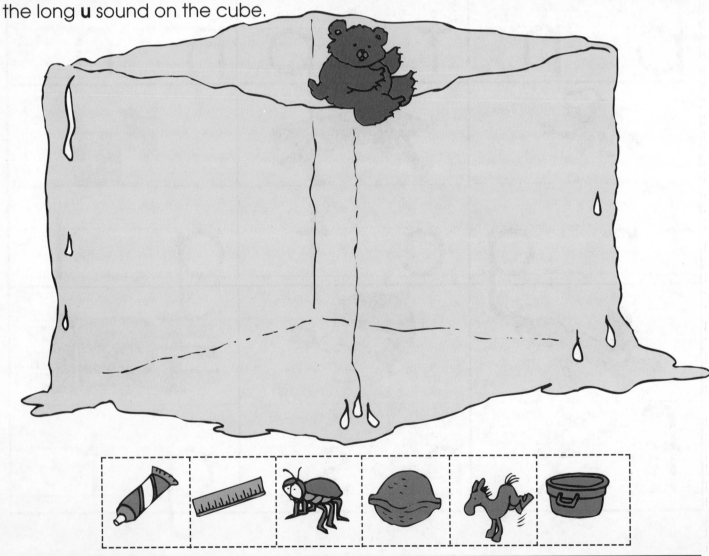

Long Vowel u

Directions: Look at the pictures. Read the words. Draw a line from each word to the picture it tells about.

cute		prune	
cube		tune	

mule		fuse	
huge		tube	

June		flute	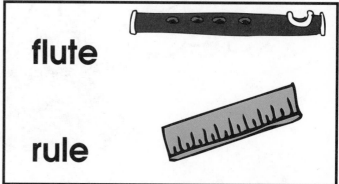
dune		rule	

Name: _____

Long Vowel e

What does the t<u>ea</u>m <u>se</u>e in the tr<u>ee</u>?

t<u>ea</u>m

tr<u>ee</u>

Directions: Long **e** is the sound you hear in the words **team** and **tree**. Say each picture name on the tree. Color the space if the picture name has the long **e** sound.

Spiders, the dark, thunder ... Write about something in nature that frightens you. What might you do to be less afraid?

Name: _____

Long Vowel e

Directions: Read each sentence. Circle the word that completes each sentence. Write the word on the line.

_____

1. We all help make the _____ . **feet   eat   meal**

2. Dad heats the _____ . **beef   mean   read**

3. Lee cleans the green _____ . **beaks   leak   beans**

4. Mom has an orange to _____ . **peas   peel   pails**

5. But where are the _____ ? **seeds   seals   leafs**

6. I will take a _____ . **poke   jeep   peek**

Name: _____

Reviewing Short and Long Vowels

Directions: Say each picture name. Circle the correct word.

cone kit kite	bed bead bike	pain pail pal	meal mug mule
cone cot coat	pine peek pin	hay hail hat	dig dog dune
hot hose hive	cup cute cave	make mail mat	feet fuse file
tub tube tune	jeep jet jam	can came cane	seal seat sail

Name: _____

ABC Order

Directions: Draw a line to connect the dots. Follow the letters in **ABC** order.

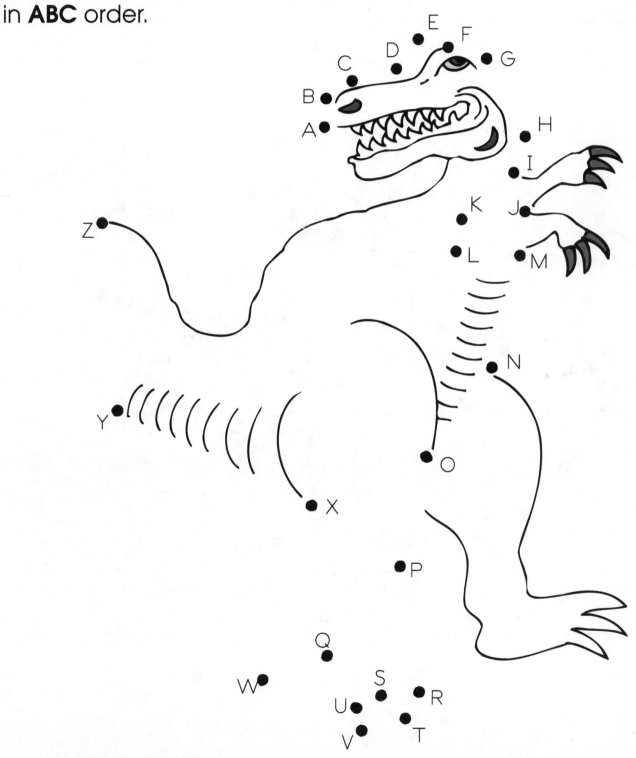

Name: _____

abc Order

Directions: Draw a line to connect the dots. Follow the letters in **abc** order.

Name: _____

Beginning Consonants Bb, Cc, Dd, Ff

Beginning consonants make the sounds that come at the beginning of words. Consonants are the letters b, c, d, f, g, h, j, k, l, m, n, p, q, r, s, t, v, w, x, y, z.

Directions: Say the name of each letter. Say the sound each letter makes. Draw a circle around the letters that make the beginning sound for each picture. Say the name of someone you know whose name begins with each letter.

Bb   Cc   Dd   Ff

Bb   Dd   Ff   Cc   Cc   Dd   Ff   Bb

Bb   Dd   Ff   Cc   Cc   Dd   Ff   Bb

Name: _____

Beginning Consonants Gg, Hh, Jj, Kk

Directions: Say the name of each letter. Say the sound that each letter makes. Then, trace the letter that makes the beginning sound in the picture. After you finish, look around the room. Name the things that start with the letters Gg, Hh, Jj, and Kk.

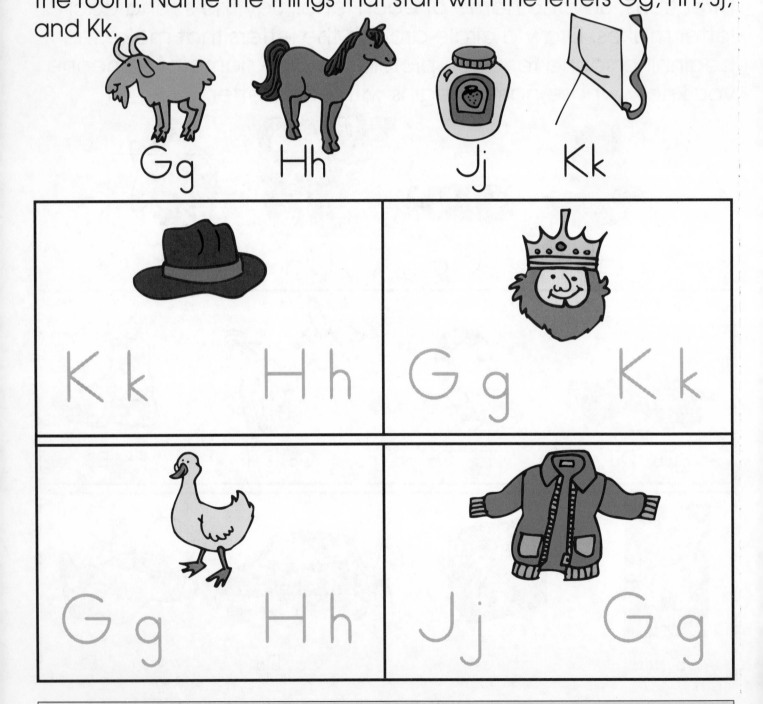

Gg   Hh   Jj   Kk

K k   H h   G g   K k

G g   H h   J j   G g

Name: _____

Beginning Consonants Ll, Mm, Nn, Pp

Directions: Say the name of each letter. Say the sound each letter makes. Then, trace the letters. Now, draw a line from each letter to the picture which begins with the letter. After you finish, say the letters Ll, Mm, Nn, Pp again.

Name: _____

Beginning Consonants Qq, Rr, Ss, Tt

Directions: Say the name of each letter. Say the sound that each letter makes. Then, trace each letter in the boxes. Color the picture which begins with the sound of the letter.

Qq   Rr   Ss   Tt

Name: _____

Beginning Consonants Vv, Ww, Xx, Yy, Zz

Directions: Say the name of each letter. Say the sound the letter makes. Then, trace the letters. Now, draw a line from the letters that match the beginning sound in each picture.

  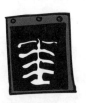  

V v   W w   X x   Y y   Z z

V v

W w

X x

Y y

Z z

Review

Directions: Help Meg and Kent and their dog, Sam, get to the magic castle. Trace all of the letters of the alphabet. Then, write the lower case consonant next to the matching upper case letter on the road to the magic castle. Make the sound for each consonant. After you finish, draw a picture on another paper of what you think Meg and Sam will find in the magic castle.

Name: _____

Ending Consonants b, d, f

Ending consonants are the sounds that come at the end of the words that are not the vowel sounds.

Directions: Say the name of each picture. Then, write b, d, or f to name the ending sound for each picture.

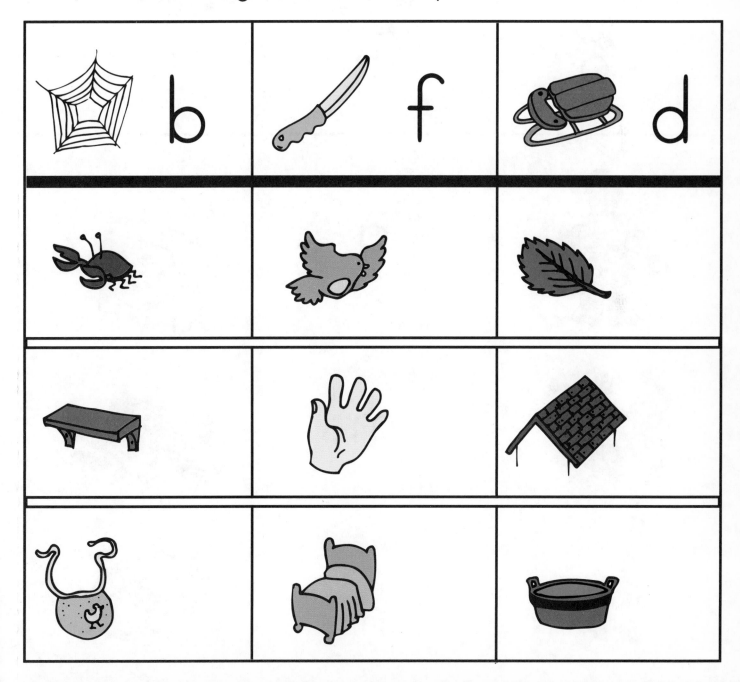

Name: _____

Ending Consonants g, m, n

Directions: Say the name of the picture. Draw a line from each letter to a picture which ends with the sound of that letter.

g

m

n

g

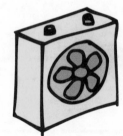

m

n

Ending Consonants k, l, p

Directions: Say the name of the pictures. Color the pictures in each row that end with the sound of the letter at the beginning of the row. Trace the letters.

Name: _____

Ending Consonants r, s, t, x

Directions: Say the name of the picture. Then circle the ending sound for each picture.

r s t x

r s t x

r s t x

r s t x

r s t x

r s t x

r s t x

r s t x

Name: _____

Beginning and Ending Sounds Discrimination

Directions: Say the name of the picture. Draw a blue circle around the picture if it begins with the sound of the letter. Draw a green triangle around the picture if it ends with the sound of the letter.

w

l

m

k

n

u

t

s

z

Name: _____

Beginning and Ending Sounds Discrimination

Directions: Say the name of each picture. Draw a triangle around the letter that makes the beginning sound. Draw a square around the letter that makes the ending sound. Color the pictures.

o r t   f d w   v t b

x c r   t g d   d a k

l m h   x g r   p t v

Name: _____

Beginning and Ending Sounds Discrimination

Directions: Look at the example. Say the beginning and ending sounds for the word **pipe**. Write the letter that makes the beginning and ending sound for each picture.

p _____  p _____   _____ _____

_____  _____   _____  _____

_____  _____   _____  _____

_____  _____   _____  _____

deiou

Name: _____

Review

Directions: Say the name of each object which has a consonant near it. Color the object orange if it begins with the sound of the letter. Color the object purple if it ends with the sound of the letter.

Name: _____

Short Vowel Sounds

The short vowel sounds used in this book are found in the following words: ant, egg, igloo, on, up.

Directions: Say the name of each picture. The short vowel sound may be in the front of the word or in the middle of the word. Color the pictures in each row that have the correct short vowel sound.

a

e

i

o

u

Name: _____

Long Vowel Sounds

Long vowel sounds say their own name. The following words have long vowel sounds: hay, me, pie, no, cute.

Directions: Say the name of each picture. Color the pictures in each row that have the correct long vowel sound.

a   

e   

i   

o   

u   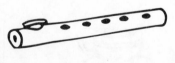

Name: _____

Discrimination Of Short And Long Aa

Directions: Say the name of each picture. If it has the short ă
sound, color it red. If it has the long ā sound, color it yellow.

ă

ā

Name: _____

Discrimination Of Short And Long Ee

Directions: Say the name of each picture. Draw a circle around the pictures which have the short **ĕ** sound. Draw a triangle around the pictures which have the long **ē** sound.

ĕ   ē

Name: _____

Discrimination Of Short And Long Ii.

Directions: Say the name of each picture. Color it yellow if it has the short **i** sound. Color it red if it has the long **ī** sound.

i̯   i̯

     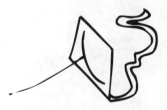

Name: ____________________

Discrimination Of Short And Long Oo

Directions: Say the name of each picture. If the picture has a long **o** sound, write a green **L** in the space. If the picture has a short **o** sound, write a red **S** in the space.

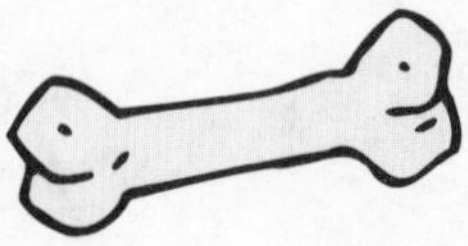

____

____

____

____

____

____

____

____

Name: _____

Discrimination Of Short And Long Uu

Directions: Say the name of the picture. If it has the long **u** sound, write a **u** in the unicorn column. If it has a short **u** sound, write a **u** in the umbrella column.

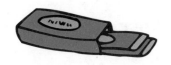   _____   _____

   _____   _____

          _____   _____

          _____   _____

          _____   _____

   _____   _____

Name: _____

Short And Long Vowel Sounds

Directions: Say the name of the picture. Write the correct vowel on each line to finish the word. Color the short vowel pictures yellow. Circle the long vowel pictures.

  j _____ g

  t _____ pe

 l _____ af

 p _____ n

 l _____ ck

 c _____ t

 c _____ be

  b _____ ll

 k _____ te

 r _____ pe

Name: _____

ABC Order

Use the first letter of each word to put the words in alphabetical order.

Directions: Draw a circle around the first letter of each word. Then, put the words in **ABC** order.

(c)ar   (b)ird

moon   two

nest   fan

bird _____

_____

car _____

card   dog

pig   bike

sun   pie

_____

_____

Name: _____

ABC Order

Directions: Circle the first letter of each animal's name. Write a 1, 2, 3, 4, 5, or 6 on the line next to the animals' names to put the words in **ABC** order.

skunk _____

dog _____

butterfly _____

zebra _____

tiger _____

fish _____

Name: _____

The Super E

When you add an **e** to some words, the vowel changes from a short vowel sound to a long vowel sound.

Example: rip + **e** = ripe.

Directions: Say the word under the first picture in each pair. Then, add an **e** to the word under the matching picture. Say the new word.

pet _____   tub _____

man _____   kit _____

pin _____   cap _____

Compound Words

Compound words are two words that are put together to make one word.

Directions: Look at the pictures and read the two words that are next to each other. Now, put the words together to make a new word. Write the new word.

Example:

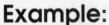 + 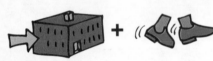 =  house boat = houseboat

 + =
side   walk

 + =
lip   stick

 =
sand   box

 + =
lunch   box

Name: _____

Synonyms

Synonyms are words that mean the same thing. **Start** and **begin** are synonyms.

Directions: Find the two words that describe each picture. Write the words in the boxes below the picture.

small funny large sad silly little big unhappy	

Name: _____

Antonyms

Antonyms are words that are opposites. **Hot** and **cold** are antonyms.

Directions: Draw a line between the words that are opposites. Can you think of other words that are opposites?

closed

below

full

empty

above

old

new

open

Name: _____

Homonyms

Homonyms are words that sound the same but are spelled differently and mean something different. **Blew** and **blue** are homonyms.

Directions: Look at the word pairs. Choose the word that describes the picture. Write the word on the line next to the picture.

1. sew   so   _____

_____

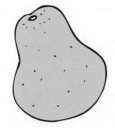

2. pair   pear   _____

_____

3. eye   I   _____

_____

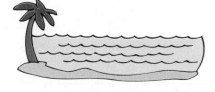

4. see   sea   _____

Name: _____

Review

Directions: Read the sentences below. Fill in the blanks with the correct word. Then circle the first letter of each word and write them in **ABC** order on the lines below.

| sunglasses | Pete | rock | cold | eight |

1. Sun + glasses = _____.

2. Another word for stone is _____.

3. The opposite word for hot is _____.

4. A word that sounds like the word ate _____.

5. Add an "e" to the word pet _____.

ABC Order: _____ _____ _____

_____ _____ _____

_____ _____

_____ _____

aeiou

Name: _____

Nouns Are Naming Words

Nouns tell the name of a person, place, or thing.

Directions: Look at each picture. Color it red if it names a person. Color it blue if it names a place. Color it green if it names a thing.

Name: _____

Nouns Are Naming Words

Directions: Write these naming words in the correct box.

| store | zoo | child | baby | teacher | table |
| cat | park | gym | woman | sock | horse |

Person

_____   _____

_____   _____

Place

_____   _____

_____   _____

Thing

_____   _____

_____   _____

Name: _____

More Than One

Some nouns name more than one person, place or thing.

Directions: Add an "s" to make the words tell about the picture.

frog___

pan___

boy___

egg___

horn___

girl___

Name: _____

More Than One

Directions: Read the nouns under the pictures. Then, write the noun under **One** or **More Than One**.

One

_____

_____

_____

_____

_____

_____

More Than One

_____

_____

_____

_____

_____

_____

barn

cows

ducks

wagon

horse

pigs

Name: _____

Verbs Are Action Words

Verbs are words that tell what a person or a thing can do.

Example: The girl pats the dog.
The word "pats" is the verb. It shows action.

Directions: Draw a line between the verbs and the pictures that show the action.

eat

run

sleep

swim

sing

hop

Verbs Are Action Words.

Directions:
Look at the pictures.
Read the words.
Write an action
word in each
sentence below.

swing
rings
kick
run
talk

1. The two boys like to _____ together.

2. The children_____ the soccer ball.

3. Some children like to _____ on the swings.

4. The girl can_____ very fast.

5. The teacher_____ the bell.

Name: _____

Is And Are Are Special Words

Use "is" when talking about one person or one thing. Use "are" when talking about more than one person or thing.

Example: The dog is barking.
                The dogs are barking.

Directions: Write "is" or "are" in the sentences below.

1. Jim_____ playing baseball.

2. Fred and Sam _____ good friends.

3. Cupcakes _____ my favorite treat.

4. Lisa _____ a good soccer player.

Name: _____

Nouns And Verbs

Directions: Read the sentences below. Draw a red circle around the nouns. Draw a blue line under the verbs.

1. The boy runs fast.

2. The turtle eats leaves.

3. The fish swim in the tank.

4. The girl hits the ball.

Name: _____

Words That Describe

Describing words tell us more about a person, place, or thing.

Directions: Read the words in the box. Choose a word that describes the picture. Write it next to the picture.

happy	round	sick	cold	long

_____

_____

_____

_____

_____

_____

_____

_____

_____

_____

Name: _____

Words That Describe

Directions: Read the words in the box. Choose the word that describes the picture. Write it on the line below.

wet	round	funny	soft	sad	tall

_____

_____

_____

_____

_____

_____

Name: _____

Words That Describe

Directions: Circle the describing word in each sentence. Draw a line from the word to the picture.

1. The hungry dog is eating.

2. The tiny bird is flying.

3. Horses have long legs.

4. She is a fast runner.

5. The little boy was lost.

Name: _____

Names Of People

The names of people begin with a capital letter.

Directions: Choose a name from the box to go with each child. Write the name on the line. Start each name with a capital letter.

Sam	Fred
Jack	Lisa
Ann	Jenny

1   **2**   **3**   **4**   **5**   **6**

1. _____ 4. _____

2. _____ 5. _____

3. _____ 6. _____

Name: _____

Name That Cat

The name of a pet begins with a capital letter.

Directions: Read the names in the box. Choose one name for each cat. Write the name in the space under the cat.

Fritz	Fuzzy	Boots	King	Queenie	Lola

_____   _____   _____

_____   _____   _____

Holidays

Holidays begin with capital letters.

Directions: Choose the words from the box to match the holiday. Write the words under the picture. Be sure to start with capital letters.

Fourth of July President's Day	Valentine's Day Thanksgiving

_____

_____

_____

_____

Name: _____

Days of the Week

The days of the week begin with capital letters.

Directions: Write the days of the week in the spaces below. Put them in order. Be sure to start with capital letters.

Tuesday

Saturday

Monday

Friday

Thursday

Sunday

Wednesday

Name: _____

Review

Directions: Circle the letters that should be capital letters.
Underline the describing words.

1. jan has red flowers for mother's day.

2. We eat a hot lunch on monday.

3. jim and fred are fast runners.

4. spot is a small dog.

5. We go to the big store on friday.

Name: _____

Telling Sentences

Sentences can tell us something. Telling sentences begin with a capital letter. They end with a period.

Directions: Read the sentences. Draw a yellow circle around the capital letter at the beginning of the sentence. Draw a purple circle around the period at the end of the sentence.

1. I am seven years old.

2. The bird is pretty.

3. The boy likes to dance.

4. Turtles like to swim.

Telling Sentences

Directions: Read the sentences. Write the sentences on the lines below. Begin each sentence with a capital letter. End each sentence with a period.

1. most children like pets
2. some children like dogs
3. some children like cats
4. some children like snakes
5. some children like all animals

1. _____

2. _____

3. _____

4. _____

5. _____

Name: _____

Telling Sentences

Directions: Read the sentences. Write the sentences below. Start each sentence with a capital letter and end with a period.

1. i like to go to the store with Mom
2. we go on Friday
3. i get to push the cart
4. i get to buy the cookies
5. i like to help Mom

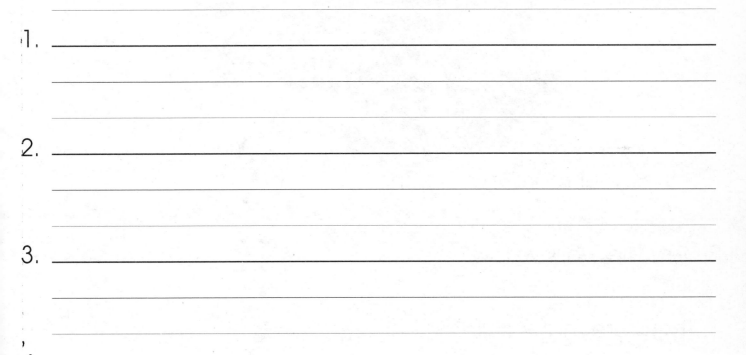

1. _____

_____

2. _____

_____

3. _____

_____

4. _____

_____

5. _____

_____

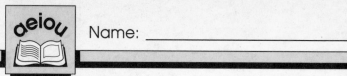

Name: _____

Asking Sentences

Asking sentences ask a question. An asking sentence begins with a capital letter. It ends with a question mark.

Directions: Draw a green line under the sentences that ask a question.

1. Does your room look like this?

2. Are the walls yellow?

3. There are many children.

4. Do you sit at desks or tables?

5. The teacher likes her job.

aeiou

Name: _____

Asking Sentences

Directions: Draw a blue line under the sentences that ask a question.

1. We like to camp.

2. Do you like to camp?

3. We like to sing at camp.

4. Can you make a fire?

5. We like to cook hot dogs.

Name: _____

Asking Sentences

Directions: Write the first word of each asking sentence. Be sure to start each question with a capital letter. End each question with a question mark.

1. _____ you like the zoo   **do**

2. _____ much does it cost   **how**

3. _____ you feed the ducks   **can**

4. _____ you see the monkeys   **will**

5. _____ time will you eat lunch   **what**

Name: _____

Periods And Question Marks

Use a period at the end of a telling sentence. Use a question mark at the end of an asking sentence.

Directions: Put a period or a question mark at the end of each sentence below.

1. Do you like a parade

2. The clowns lead the parade

3. Can you hear the band

4. The balloons are big

5. Can you see the horses

Name: _____

Review

Directions: Look at the picture. In the space below, write one telling sentence about the picture. Then, write one asking sentence about the picture.

A telling sentence.

_____

_____

An asking sentence.

_____

_____

Name: _____

Word Order

Word order is the logical order of words in a sentence.

Directions: Put the words in each sentence in order. Write the sentence on the lines.

1. We made lemonade. some
2. good. It was
3. We the sold lemonade.
4. cost It five cents.
5. <u>fun. We had</u>

1. _____

2. _____

3. _____

4. _____

5. _____

Name: _____

Word Order

Directions: Look at the picture. Put the words in the correct order. Write the sentences on the lines below.

1. a Jan starfish. has
2. and Bill to Peg swim. like
3. The shining. sun is
4. sand. the in Jack likes play to
5. cold. water The is

1. _____

_____

2. _____

_____

3. _____

_____

4. _____

_____

5. _____

_____

Name: _____

Word Order Can Change Meaning

If you change the order of the words in a sentence, you can change the meaning of the sentence.

Directions: Read the sentences. Draw a purple circle around the sentence that describes the picture.

Example:

The fox jumped over the dogs.

The dogs jumped over the fox.

1. The cat watched the bird.
   The bird watched the cat.

2. The girl looked at the boy.
   The boy looked at the girl.

3. The turtle ran past the rabbit.
   The rabbit ran past the turtle.

Name: _____

I Can Write Sentences

A story has more than one sentence.

Directions: Use the words from the pictures to write a story.

girl

boy

play

books

swing

school

I am a happy _____ . I go to _____ .

I like to read _____ . I like to _____

on the playground. I like to _____ on the swings.

Name: _____

I Can Write Sentences

Directions: Draw a picture of yourself in the box marked **Me**. Then write three sentences about yourself on the lines.

Me

1. _____

2. _____

3. _____

Name: _____

Review

Directions: Put the words in the right order to make a sentence. The sentences will tell a story.

1. a gerbil. has Ann
2. is The Mike. named gerbil
3. likes eat. Mike to
4. play. to Mike likes
5. happy a is gerbil. Mike

_____

1. _____

_____

2. _____

_____

3. _____

_____

4. _____

_____

5. _____

_____

In My Home

Do this with a grown-up.
Look around your home.

Mitt begins with the same sound as **moon.**

Find something that begins with the same sound as <u>run</u>.

Find something that begins with the same sound as <u>ball</u>.

Write its name. _____
Draw a picture of what you named.

Write its name. _____
Draw a picture of what you named.

Find something that ends with the same sound as <u>wet</u>.

Find something that ends with the same sound as <u>good</u>.

Write its name. _____
Draw a picture of what you named.

Write its name. _____
Draw a picture of what you named.

Suitcases

Do this with a grown-up.

Help the Green family pack for a trip.

Take turns.

Draw a line from each person to things
he or she will pack.

Mom will pack things with names that begin with
the same sound as <u>mop</u>.

Dad will pack things with names that begin with
the same sound as <u>pig</u>.

Pat will pack things with names that end with
the same sound as <u>look</u>.

Bill will pack things with names that end with
the same sound as <u>well</u>.

Toss a Word

Play this game with a grown-up.

Get a penny and toss it on the game board.

Look at the letter in the space where the penny lands.

Try to use the letter to finish a word on your
Word Card.

Write the letter in the word.

Take turns.

To win, you must fill in your Word Card first.

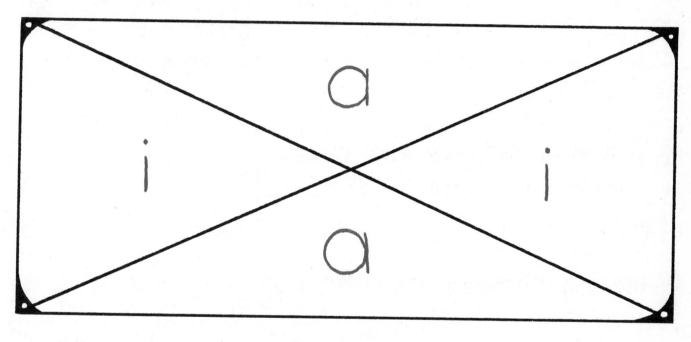

My Word Card

| l___p | d___g | r___b | c___p | f___n | m___p |

My Grown-up's Word Card

| l___p | d___g | r___b | c___p | f___n | m___p |

Make a Word

Play this game with a grown-up.

Make letter cards like these.

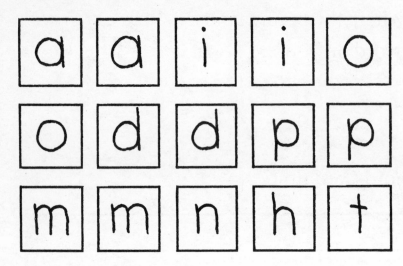

Turn over the cards.

Pick 3 cards.

Try to use the letters to make a real word.

Write the word on your Word Board.

Then turn your cards back over.

Take turns.

The first player to make 3 different words wins.

My Word Board	My Grown-up's Word Board

Do They Sound the Same?

Play this game with a grown-up.
Make word cards like these.

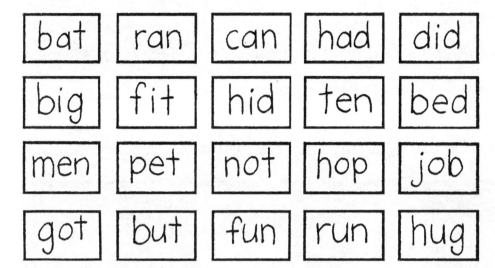

bat	ran	can	had	did
big	fit	hid	ten	bed
men	pet	not	hop	job
got	but	fun	run	hug

Turn over the cards.

Pick 2 cards.

Read the words on the cards out loud.

Listen for the vowel sounds.

If the words have the same vowel sound,

keep the cards.

If the words do not have the same vowel sound,

turn the cards back over.

Take turns.

Play until no more cards are left.

Then count your cards.

How many cards do you have? _____

How many cards does your grown-up have? _____

The player with more cards wins the game.

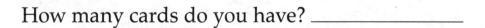

Word Checkers

Play this game with a grown-up.

Make 8 small red markers.

Put them on the two bottom rows of words.

Have your grown-up make 8 small blue markers.

Put them on the two top rows of words.

Then play checkers, but with one difference.

Read the word in a box before you put a marker on it.

	to		do		has		of
let		as		so		fly	
	us		for		be		old
two		now		who		way	
	get		me		by		yes
up		had		her		him	
	but		old		saw		day

Which Is Better?

Do this with a grown-up.

Read the words in the first box.

Put an **X** under the name of the thing you like better.

Put a ✔ under the name of the thing your grown-up likes better.

Do the rest of the boxes the same way.

apple or banana	milk or juice	lions or tigers

elephants or bears	trees or flowers	winter or summer

airplanes or trains	cars or trucks	orange or green

Make up 2 more sets of words.

Put an **X** under the names of the things you like better.

_____ or _____   _____ or _____

Fill the Balloons

Play this game with a grown-up.

Toss a coin on the game board.

Read the words in the box where the coin lands.

If the words have the same or almost the same meaning, color 2 of your balloons.

If the words have opposite meanings, color 1 balloon.

Take turns.

You win if you color all your balloons first.

happy	on	little	more
sad	off	small	less
nice	silly	up	below
mean	funny	down	under

My Balloons

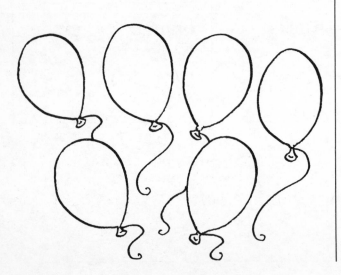

My Grown-up's Balloons

Name: _____

Beginning Consonants

Directions: Look at the letters on the blocks. Say each picture name. On the line, write the letter or letters from the blocks that stand for the sound you hear at the **beginning** of the picture name.

When you clean your closet, what might you do with the toys that you have outgrown?

Name: _____

Beginning Consonants

Directions: Say the name of each animal in the pet store. On the line, write the letter that stands for the sound you hear at the **beginning** of the picture name.

Which of these animals would you like to have as a pet?
What will you name your pet?
What will you buy at the pet store to help you take care of it?

Name: _____

Ending Consonants

Directions: Say the name of each animal at the zoo. On the line, write the letter that stands for the sound you hear at the **end** of the picture name.

W | Imagine that you are the zookeeper at this zoo.
What will you tell visitors about the zoo and its animals?

Phonics

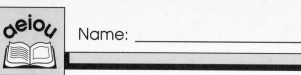

Name: _____

Middle Consonants

The letter **d** stands for the sound you hear in the middle of the word **ladder**.

Directions: Say each picture name. On the line, write the letter that stands for the sound you hear in the **middle** of the picture name.

Why do you think the ladder is propped against the tree?

234

Name: _____

Beginning, Middle, and Ending Consonants

Directions: Say each picture name. In the spaces below the picture, write the letters that stand for the sounds you hear at the beginning, middle, and end of the picture name. The first one shows you what to do.

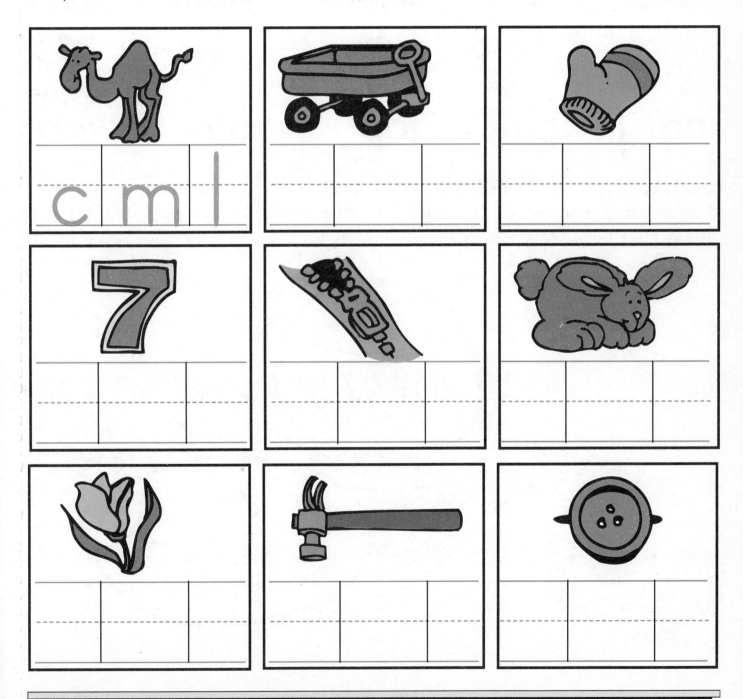

Name: _____

Short Vowels

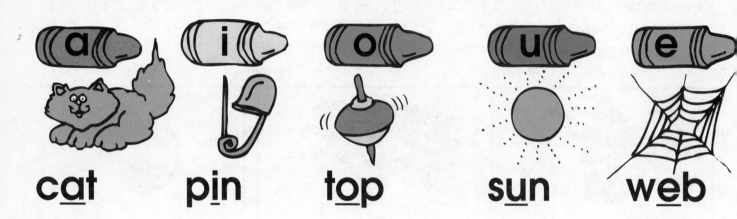

c**a**t p**i**n t**o**p s**u**n w**e**b

Directions: Say each picture name on pages 8 and 9. Listen to the short vowel sound. Find the letter that stands for the vowel sound on a crayon. Use your crayons to make the balloons the right color.

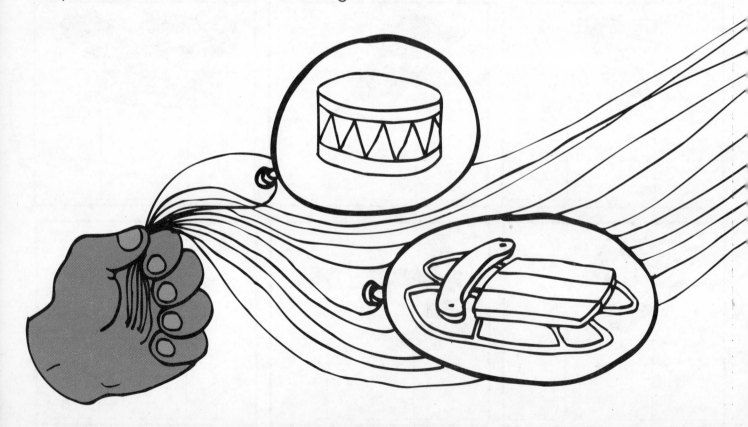

aeiou

Name: _____

Name: _____

Short Vowels

Directions: Say the name of each picture. Circle the picture name. Write the name. The first one shows you what to do.

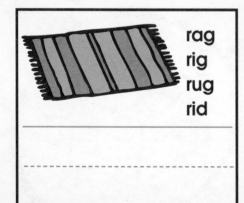 hit / hot / (hat) / hug — **hat**	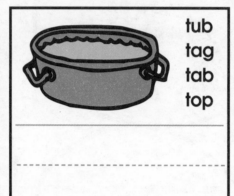 tub / tag / tab / top	 fit / fat / fix / fox
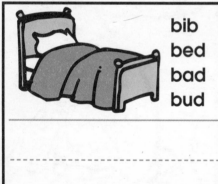 bib / bed / bad / bud	 wit / wag / wig / wet	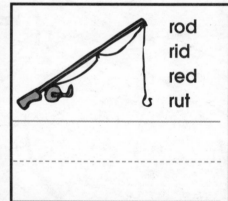 rod / rid / red / rut
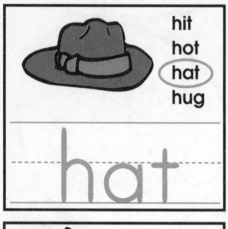 rag / rig / rug / rid	 lap / lid / lad / lit	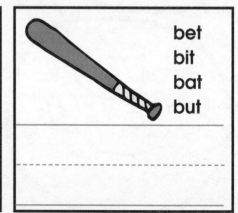 bet / bit / bat / but

Name: _____

A Plan for Reading

Directions: Read this sentence:

Can Dad get the big box off the bus?

Look at the letters in each underlined word. The letters in each word follow the same pattern. To find the letter pattern, circle the word that will complete each sentence.

1. The first letter in each word is a

   consonant

   vowel

2. The second letter in each word is a

   consonant

   vowel

3. The third letter in each word is a

   consonant

   vowel

Read the words you circled. The letter pattern in the underlined words is called **consonant-vowel-consonant** or the **CVC** pattern. Words with the CVC pattern usually have a short vowel sound. Knowing about the CVC pattern gives you a plan for figuring out new words.

A Plan for Reading

When you come to a new word with the **CVC** letter pattern,
try the **short vowel** sound.
Then read the sentence again to be sure the word makes sense.

Write more about the big box. Who sent it? Why?
What will Dad do next?

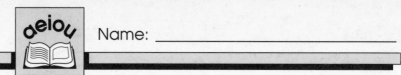

Review Consonants and Short Vowels

Directions: Write the picture name on the line.

Name: _____

Review Consonants and Short Vowels

Directions: Read each sentence. Draw a picture of what the sentence tells about.

Peg has six nuts in a box.

Ten bugs sat on a big log.

Directions: Now write a sentence that tells about the picture below.

_____

- -

_____

- -

_____

Name: _____

Exploring Rhyming Words

A Ferris wheel is lots of **fun**.
You feel like you can touch the **sun**!

Directions: Words like **fun** and **sun** are called rhyming words because they have the same ending sounds. Cut out the wheels. Put the little wheel on top of the big Ferris wheel. Push a straw or a ballpoint pen through the center. Turn the little wheel. How many rhyming words can you make? List the words you make on a separate sheet of paper.

Diagram:

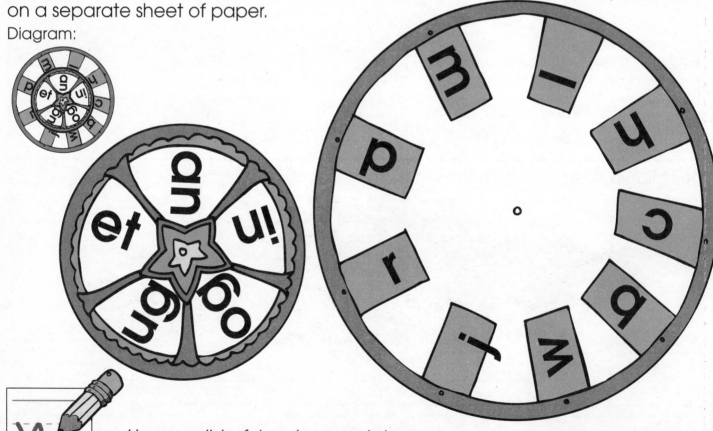

Use your list of rhyming words to
write a short rhyme about something you think is fun to do.

Name: _____

Rhyming Words

Directions: Read each riddle. Write the answer on the line. Then write two words that rhyme with the answer. The first one shows you what to do.

We carry groceries in it. It holds books or our lunch, too. What is it?

bag   rag   tag

It likes to dig in the mud. It has a curly tail. What is it?

_____   b_____   w_____

It is the number of our fingers. It is the number of our toes too! What is it?

_____   m_____   p_____

Bunnies can do this. So can kangaroos and frogs. What is it?

_____   m_____   t_____

Make up a riddle about one of the rhyming words.
Ask a friend to solve it.

Name: _____

Long Vowels

Directions: Say each picture name on pages 16 and 17. Listen to the long vowel sound. Find the letter that stands for the long vowel sound on a crayon. Use your crayons to make the leaves the right color.

aeiou

Name: _____

Name: _____

Long Vowel a

Help J<u>ay</u> s<u>ai</u>l across the l<u>a</u>k<u>e</u> to the c<u>a</u>v<u>e</u>.

Directions: Long **a** is the sound you hear in the words **Jay**, **sail**, and **lake**. Read the words on Jay's sail. Then look at the pictures on the maze. Use the words on the sail to label the pictures on the maze. The first one shows you what to do.

vase	mail	hay
cake	tray	rain
	tape	pay
	pail	

Write about an adventure Jay has when he gets to the cave.

Name: _____

Long Vowel i

I l<u>i</u>k<u>e</u> this gift best.
And that's no l<u>ie</u>.

Directions: Long **i** is the sound you hear in the words **like** and **lie**. Read each word below. Find out what gift Dad likes best by coloring the space if the word has the **long i** sound.

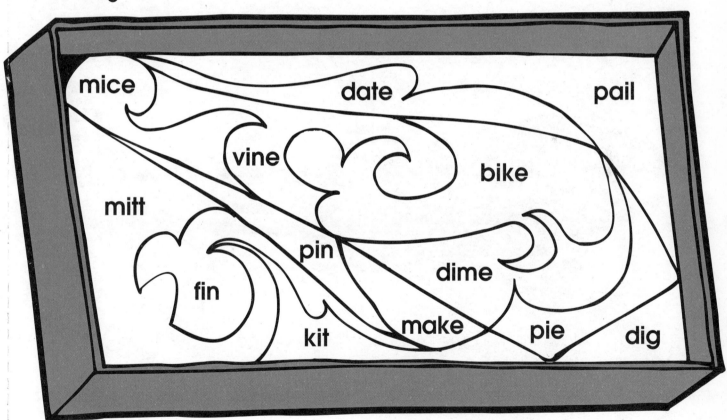

mice date pail
vine bike
mitt
pin dime
fin
kit make pie dig

Think about the best gift you ever received.
Why was it your favorite?

Name: _____

Long Vowel u

The c<u>u</u>te m<u>u</u>le pulls a cart to the village.

Directions: Long **u** is the sound you hear in the words **cute** and **mule**. Read the words at the bottom of the page. Cut them out. If the word has the **long u** sound, paste it on the cart. Then draw a little picture that goes with each word.

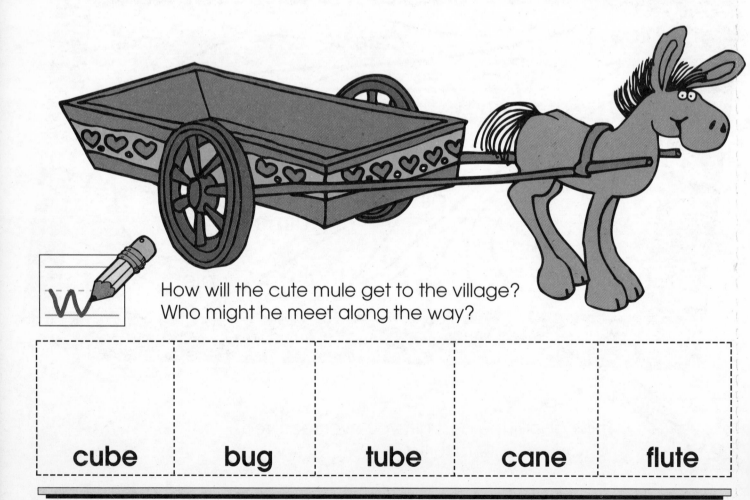

How will the cute mule get to the village?
Who might he meet along the way?

| cube | bug | tube | cane | flute |

Name: _____

Long Vowel o

J<u>oe</u> used a c<u>oa</u>t, a b<u>ow</u>, and a carrot for the n<u>o</u>s<u>e</u>.

Directions: Long **o** is the sound you hear in the words **Joe, coat, bow,** and **nose.** Cut out the flash cards. Sort them by different spellings for the sound of **long o**. Read each word. Then make up a game to play with the cards.

toe	**soap**	**goat**	**rope**
mow	**hoe**	**bone**	**row**

Name: _____

Long Vowel o

Imagine that lots and lots of snow has just fallen. What will you do in all that snow?

Name: _____

Long Vowel e

Take a s<u>ea</u>t in the j<u>ee</u>p.

Directions: Long **e** is the sound you hear in the words **seat** and **jeep**. Take a ride in the jeep to see an animal that is the symbol of the United States. Follow the path that has **long e** words to find out which animal it is.

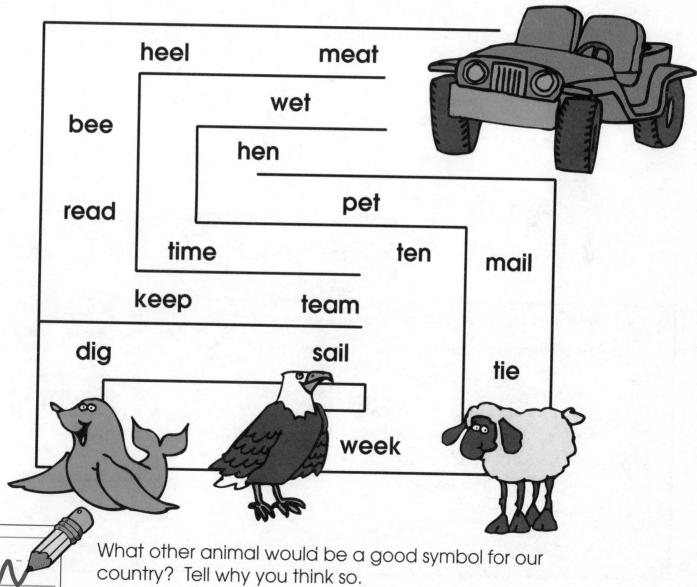

heel   meat
wet
bee   hen
read   pet
time   ten   mail
keep   team
dig   sail   tie
week

What other animal would be a good symbol for our country? Tell why you think so.

Name: _____

Exploring Short and Long Vowels

cap + e = cape

Directions: Adding **e** to the end of the short vowel word **cap** changes it to the long vowel word **cape.** Cut out the tub and the water. Cut on the dotted lines to make slits. Slip the water through the slits in the tub. Next, cut out the tube. Paste the tube in the tub, but don't paste the cap down.

When the cap is on the tube, read the short vowel word. Then, fold the cap back to show the **e**. Read the long vowel word.

Diagram:

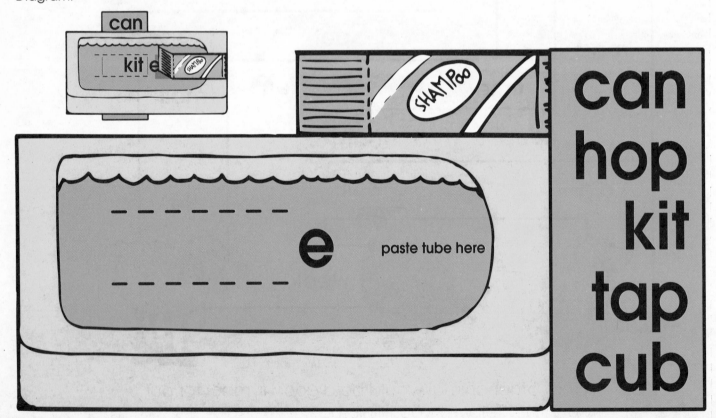

paste tube here

can
hop
kit
tap
cub

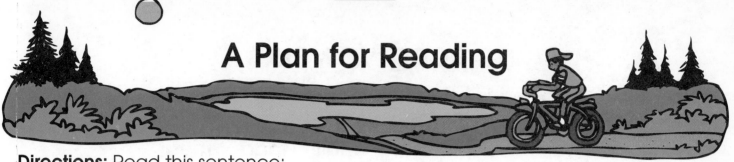

A Plan for Reading

Directions: Read this sentence:

In <u>June</u>, <u>Pete</u> <u>rode</u> his <u>bike</u> to the <u>lake</u>.

Look at the letters in each underlined word. The letters in each word follow the same pattern. To find the letter pattern, circle the correct answer.

1. The first letter in each word is a
    consonant
    vowel .

2. The second letter in each word is a
    consonant
    vowel .

3. The third letter in each word is a
    consonant
    vowel .

4. The fourth letter in each word is the
    consonant e
    vowel e .

Read the words you circled. The letter pattern in the underlined words is called **consonant-vowel-consonant-e** or the **CVCe** pattern. In words with the **CVCe** pattern, the first vowel is usually long and the final **e** is silent. Knowing about the CVCe pattern gives you a plan for figuring out new words.

A Plan for Reading

When you come to a new word with the **CVCe** letter pattern,
try the **long vowel** sound.
Then read the sentence again to be sure the word makes sense.

Name: _____

Long Vowels

Directions: Read the words in the box. Use the words to find the name of each picture. Write the name on the line.

rain	soap	seal	mail	toad	meat

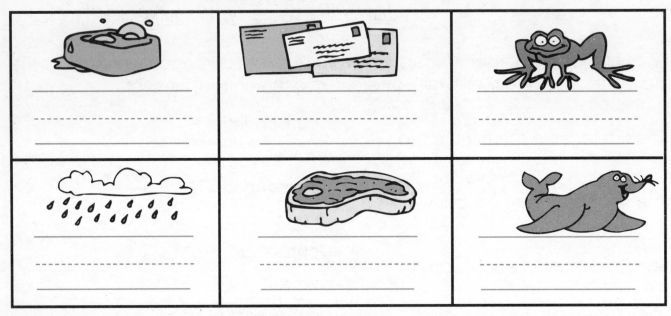

_____   _____   _____

_____   _____   _____

Directions: Find the word in the box that belongs in each sentence. Write the word on the line.

seat	load	paid	wait

1. Jean _____ for a ticket.

2. Then she had to _____ in line.

3. Soon they will _____ the coaster.

4. Will she get the front _____?

Name: _____

A Plan for Reading

Directions: Read this sentence:

We <u>tied</u> our <u>boat</u> next to a <u>pail</u>.

Look at the letters in each underlined word. The letters in each word follow the same pattern. To find the letter pattern, circle the word that will complete the sentence.

1. The first letter in each word is a

    consonant

    vowel .

2. The second letter in each word is a

    consonant

    vowel .

3. The third letter in each word is a

    consonant

    vowel .

4. The fourth letter in each word is a

    consonant

    vowel .

Read the words you circled. The letter pattern in the underlined words is called **consonant-vowel-vowel-consonant** or the **CVVC** pattern. In words with the CVVC pattern, the first vowel is usually long and the second vowel is silent. Knowing about the CVVC pattern gives you a plan for figuring out new words.

A Plan for Reading
When you come to a word with the **CVVC** letter pattern,
try the **long** sound of the first vowel.
Then read the sentence again to be sure the word makes sense.

Name: _____

Review Long Vowels

Directions: Find the word in the box that will complete each sentence. Write the word on the line.

pail	sheep	nine	bone	pie	tune	play

1. Little Tommy Tucker sang a _____ for his supper.

2. Old Mother Hubbard went to get her poor dog a _____ .

3. Little Jack Horner got a plum from a sweet _____ .

4. Mary's lamb made the children laugh and _____ .

5. Bo Peep's lost _____ came home wagging their tails.

6. Jack and Jill went up a hill to get a _____ of water.

7. The pease porridge was _____ days old.

Did you notice that the sentences above are about nursery rhymes? Work with someone to find the rhyme each sentence is about. Write one of the rhymes you remember.

Review Short and Long Vowels

Can a bug wiggle its toe? No!

Directions: Read each sentence. Circle the answer.

1. Will a fox wear a tie? **yes no**

2. Can a mule sit in a pail? **yes no**

3. Will a pig dig in the mud? **yes no**

4. Can a seal help mow hay? **yes no**

5. Will a bee buzz in its hive? **yes no**

6. Will a cat run for a bone? **yes no**

7. Can a goat eat a bag of oats? **yes no**

8. Will a hen dive into a lake? **yes no**

Write a comic about a funny animal like the bug that tried to wiggle its toes.

Name: _____

Final y as a Vowel

Our puppy stays dry in the yard.

You know that **y** is a consonant. When **y** is at the beginning of a word, it stands for the sound at the beginning of **yard**.

Did you know that **y** can be a vowel too?

Sometimes **y** can stand for the **long e** sound at the end of **puppy**. Try this sound when **y** is the only vowel at the end of a word with more than one syllable or part.

Sometimes **y** can stand for the **long i** sound at the end of **dry**. Try this sound when **y** is the only vowel at the end of a one syllable word.

Directions: Say each picture name. Circle the word that names the picture. If **y** stands for the **long e** sound in **puppy**, color the picture **brown**. If **y** stands for the **long i** sound in **dry**, color the picture **orange**.

bail
bay
baby

crazy
cry
crate

bunt
bunny
buy

fry
frosty
frog

pay
pry
pony

fly
feed
fussy

Name: _____

Final y as a Vowel

Directions: Find the word in the box that completes each sentence. Write it on the line.

funny	my	try	sunny	ninety	sky

1. Today is _____ and hot, hot, hot!

2. There isn't a cloud in the _____.

3. It feels like _____ degrees in the shade!

4. I must _____ to beat the heat.

5. I will use _____ wagon and a hose.

6. I look _____ but it works!

What is the hottest day you can remember? How did you beat the heat when you were outdoors?

Name: _____

Hard and Soft c

Get ready to <u>race</u> through the <u>city</u>!
Who will win the <u>fancy</u> shirt? Who will win the <u>cake</u>?

The letter **c** can stand for two different sounds.

You hear the **hard sound** of **c** at the beginning of **cake**.

You hear the **soft sound** of **c** in **race**, **city**, and **fancy**.
When **c** is followed by **e, i,** or **y,** try the soft sound.

Directions: Find out what Connie wins by coloring the prints with the words with the **hard c** sound yellow. Find out what Cindy wins by coloring the prints with the **soft c** sound blue.

Name: _____

Hard and Soft g

Look! There's a <u>gentle</u> <u>giant</u> on my <u>gym</u> by the <u>garden</u>.

The letter **g** can stand for two different sounds.

You hear the **hard sound** of g at the beginning of **garden**.

You hear the **soft sound** of g at the beginning of **gentle, giant,** and **gym**. When **g** is followed by **e, i,** or **y**, try the soft sound.

Directions: Use what you know about the sounds of the letter **g** to read more about the giant. Draw a picture to go with each sentence.

The giant had a magic egg.	**One day a huge goose saw the egg by the gate.**

Finish the story about the giant, the goose, and the magic egg.

S Blends

The sounds you hear at the beginning of these words are consonant blends:

<u>st</u>icks   <u>str</u>ing   <u>sp</u>oon   <u>sw</u>im   <u>sn</u>ail   <u>sl</u>eep

Directions: Say the name of each picture. Print the letters that stand for the blend you hear at the beginning.

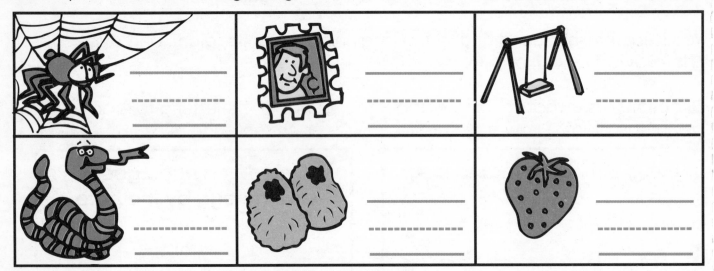

Directions: Circle the name of each picture.

smile	stop	skunk
soap	steps	skirt
smoke	strap	soak
spring	slip	screen
spot	side	scale
spray	slide	sail

S Blends

Directions: Read the words in the box. Then look at the picture. Use the words in the box to label the picture. The first one shows you what to do.

| snow | scarf | sweater | skates | sled | squirrel |

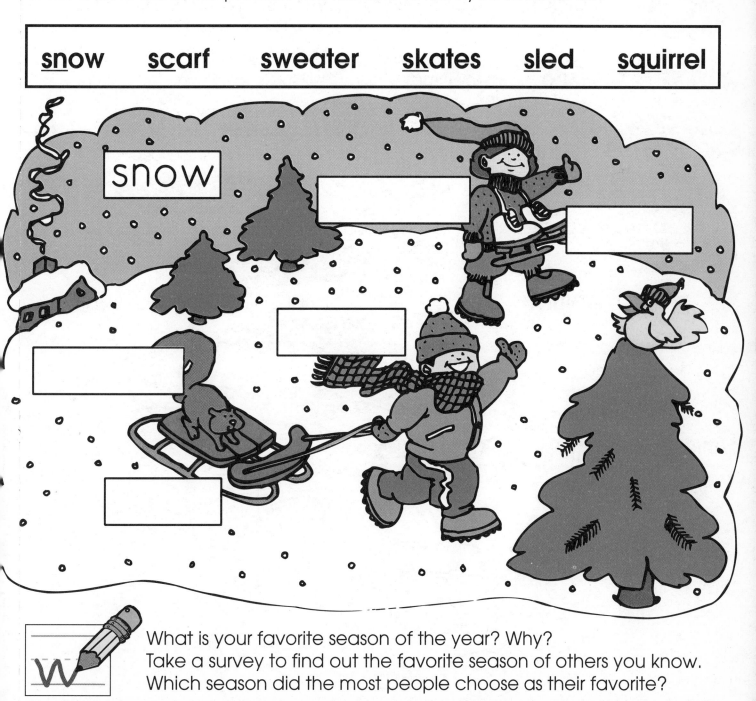

What is your favorite season of the year? Why?
Take a survey to find out the favorite season of others you know.
Which season did the most people choose as their favorite?

Name: _____

L Blends

Directions:

 clock   If you hear the sounds that the letters **cl** stand for, color the picture **red**.

 **flute**   If you hear the sounds that the letters **fl** stand for, color the picture **yellow**.

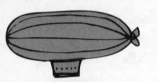 **blimp**   If you hear the sounds that the letters **bl** stand for, color the picture **orange**.

 globe   If you hear the sounds that the letters **gl** stand for, color the picture **brown**.

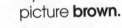

 plum   If you hear the sounds that the letters **pl** stand for, color the picture **green**.

Name: _____

L Blends

Directions: Use the words in the box to complete the sentences about the picture above.

blue	clap	float	glue	please	flag

_____ help us get ready for the parade.

Our first job is to build a _____ out of wire.

Next we will _____ paper to the sides.

We hope the sky is _____ on parade day.

We will wave the United States _____

Everyone will _____ as we pass by.

List some places where you have seen the United States flag. Why do you think people feel proud when they see our flag?

Name: _____

R Blends

Read each word. Listen for the blend at the beginning of each word.

<u>tr</u>ee   <u>dr</u>ess   <u>br</u>ead   <u>cr</u>own   <u>fr</u>og   <u>gr</u>apes   <u>pr</u>ice

Directions: Look at the letters on the presents. Find the pictures below that begin with the sounds that the letters stand for. Paste them where they belong.

dr   br   gr   pr

cr   fr   tr

Name: _____

R Blends

Directions: Use each word in the box to complete the puzzle.

brick	drain	crab	train	prize

Across

2. You might win it.

4. It runs on a track.

5. It lives by the sea.

Down

1. It is a hole in a sink.

3. You might build with it.

Make up a crossword puzzle using words with blends at the beginnings. Ask a friend to solve your puzzle.

Exploring Consonant Blends

Directions: Cut out the train and the smoke. Cut on the dotted lines to make slits. Slip the smoke through the slits on the train. Slide the smoke and read each new word.

Diagram:

Name: _____

Review Consonant Blends

Directions: Read each sentence. Circle the word that completes each sentence. Write the word on the line.

1. I like to sit and _____ about what I want to be.

   dream
   stream
   clean

2. I might let drivers know when to _____ .

   fry
   plant
   stop

3. I could teach children to read and _____ .

   sleep
   spell
   street

4. It would be fun to own a _____ .

   store
   step
   flame

5. Maybe I will be a big movie _____ .

   plant
   dress
   star

6. That dream really makes me _____ !

   smile
   grill
   small

What do you dream you might do someday?

Name: _____

Beginning Consonant Digraphs

Let's visit the <u>chicks</u> and <u>sheep</u> at the petting farm.

chicks

sheep

The letters you see at the beginning of the words **chicks** and **sheep** are called consonant digraphs. The two consonants go together to stand for one sound.

Directions: Cut out the pictures at the bottom. Say each picture name. If the picture name begins with the same sound as **chicks**, paste it near the chicks. If the picture name begins with the same sound as **sheep**, paste it near the sheep.

What do you think of this?
All petting farms are good places for animals to live.

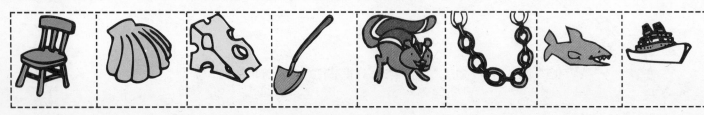

Beginning Consonant Digraphs

Thirteen swimmers saw the huge whale.

13

thirteen

whale

Directions: Say each picture name. If you hear the first sound in **thirteen**, write **th** on the line. Write **wh** if you hear the first sound in **whale.**

What would you do if you saw a whale in the ocean?
What would you do if you saw a whale stranded on the beach?

Name: _____

Final Consonant Digraphs

Jo<u>sh</u> looks at the clo<u>ck</u>.

Directions: Write the picture name on the line.

_____

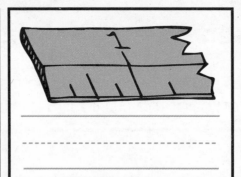

_____

_____

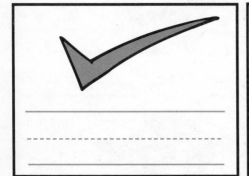

_____

_____

_____

_____

_____

_____

Name: _____

A Plan for Reading

Directions: Read this sentence:

What <u>luck</u>! We found the <u>lost</u> <u>sock</u>!

Look at the letters in each underlined word. The letters in each word follow the same pattern. To find the letter pattern, circle the word that will complete each sentence.

1. The first letter in each word is a   **consonant**   .
   vowel

2. The second letter in each word is a   **consonant**   .
   vowel

3. The third letter in each word is a   **consonant**   .
   vowel

4. The fourth letter in each word is a   **consonant**   .
   vowel

Read the words you circled. The letter pattern in the underlined words is called **consonant-vowel-consonant-consonant** or **CVCC** pattern. Words with the CVCC pattern usually have a short vowel sound. Knowing about the CVCC pattern gives you a plan for figuring out new words.

A Plan for Reading
When you come to a new word with the **CVCC** letter pattern,
try the **short vowel** sound.
Then read the sentence again to be sure the word makes sense.

Name: _____

Review Consonant Digraphs

Directions: Read the words in the box. Then look at the picture. Use the words in the box to label the picture. The first one shows you what to do.

chimney	shed	wheel	thimble
shoes	path	rock	

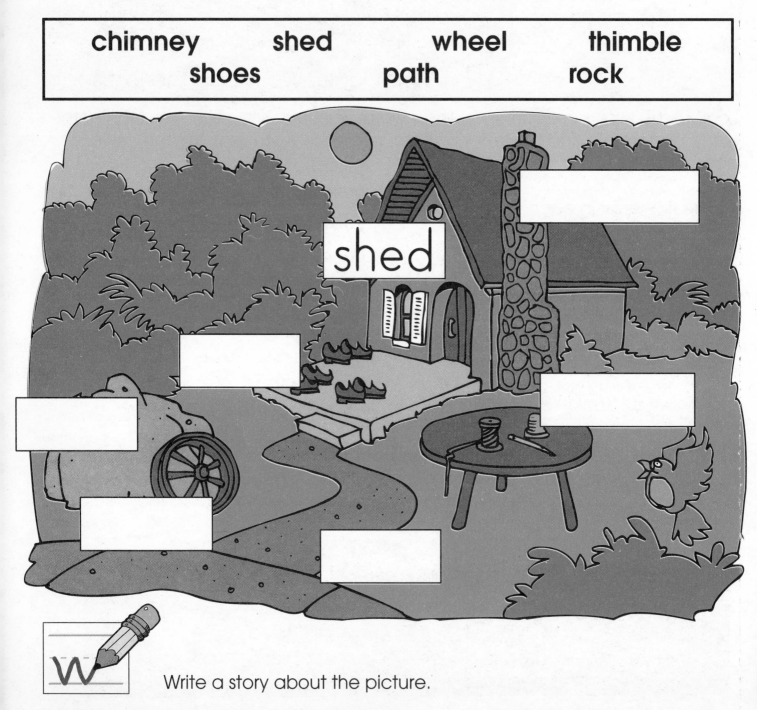

Write a story about the picture.

Name: ______________________

Review Your Plans for Reading

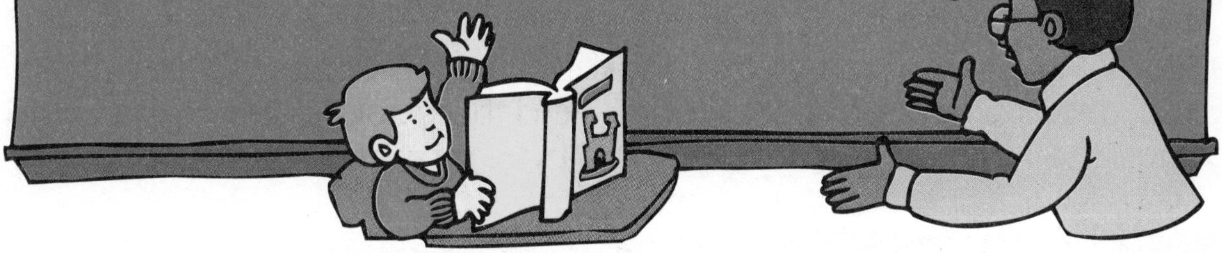

Directions: Write the underlined words under the correct letter pattern. The first one shows you what to do.

Tom began to moan, "It will take me a long time to read this good book. I'd like to be able to read all the words by myself. I can't wait to see what happens next!"

"You **can** do it," Mr. Jet reminded him. "There are many ways to figure out new words on your own. One way is to look for letter patterns."

CVC	CVCC	CVCe	CVVC
Tom			

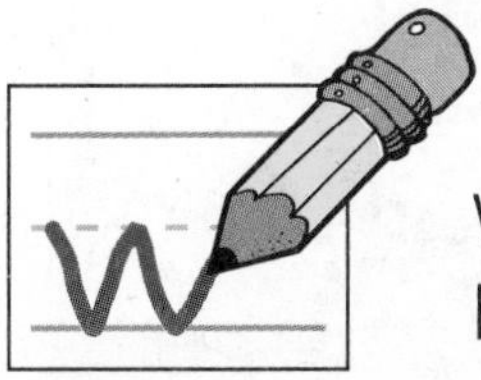

What do you think of this?
Phonics can help me be a better reader and speller.

Name: _____

Use Your Plans for Reading

Directions: Write the words on the books above the correct letter pattern on the bookmark. Cut out the bookmark. Fold the bookmark on the dotted line and tape the sides. As you read, use the bookmark to help you remember the four plans for figuring out new words.

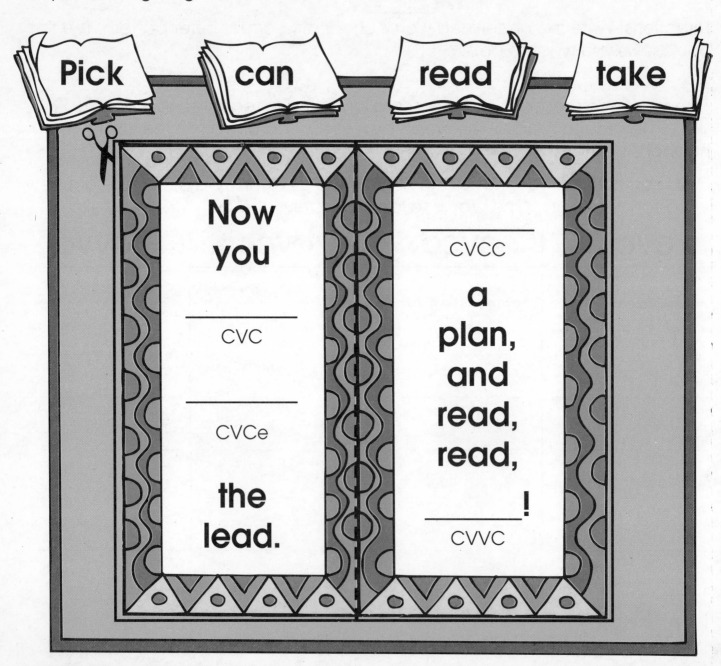

Pick   can   read   take

Now
you

_____
CVC

_____
CVCe

the
lead.

_____
CVCC

a
plan,
and
read,
read,
_____!
CVVC

Name: _____

What You Need to Know About Taking Tests

You can get better at taking tests. Here are some tips.

Do your schoolwork. Study in school. Do your homework all the time. These things will help you in school and on any tests you take. Learn new things a little at a time. Then you will remember them better when you see them on a test.

Feel your best. Get a good night's sleep. Eat a healthy breakfast.

Be ready for the test. Do practice questions. Learn about the different kinds of questions. Books like this one will help you.

Follow the test directions. Listen carefully to the directions your teacher gives. Read all instructions carefully. Watch out for words such as *not, none, never, all*, and *always*. These words can change the meaning of the directions. You may want to circle words like these. This will help you keep them in mind as you answer the questions.

Look carefully at each page before you start. Do reading tests in a special order. First, read the directions. Read the questions next. This way you will know what to look for as you read. Then read the story. Last, read the story again quickly. Skim it to find the best answer.

Use your time wisely. Many tests have time limits. Look at the clock when the test starts. Figure out when you need to stop. When you begin, look over the whole thing. Do the easy parts first. Go back and do the hard parts last. Make sure you do not spend too much time on any one part. This way, if you run out of time, you still have completed much of the test.

Sometimes it's good to guess. Here's what to do. Each question may have four or five answer choices. You may know that two answers are wrong, but you are not sure about the rest. Then make your best guess. If you are not sure about any of the answers, skip it. Do not guess. Tests like these take away extra points for wrong answers. So it is better to leave them blank.

Name: _____

What You Need to Know About Taking Tests

Check your work. You may finish the test before the time is up. Then you can go back and check your answers. Make sure you answered each question you could. Also, make sure that you filled in only one answer circle for each question. Erase any extra marks on the page.

To answer multiple choice questions:

• Answer easy questions first.

• Skip hard questions. Come back to them later. Circle the question to remember which ones you still need to do.

To answer fill-in-the-blank questions:

• Try to think of the answer before you look at the choices.

• See if one of the choices matches your answer.

To answer oral questions:

• Listen to the directions.

• Say each answer to yourself. Listen to the sounds.

• Look at all the words. Then mark the one you think is correct.

When you choose a picture to answer a question on a test:

• Listen to the story carefully.

• Try to imagine what is happening. Choose the picture that is closest to what you imagine.

• Change your answer only if you are sure it is wrong and another one is right.

Name: _____

Test-Taking Practice: Grade K

Directions: Listen for the word that means almost the same as the underlined word. Fill in the circle next to your answer.

1 <u>delicious</u> pizza

○ boring

○ hungry

○ tasty

2 <u>below</u> the desk

○ above

○ behind

○ under

3 I am afraid of <u>mice</u>.

○ bears

○ rice

○ moose

4 I like to eat spaghetti <u>dinner</u>.

○ winner

○ supper

○ finger

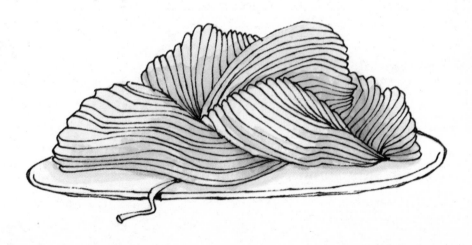

Name: _____

Test-Taking Practice: Grade K

Directions: Listen to an adult read the sentences and choices. Fill in the circle next to the answer that best completes the sentence.

1 **The cereal is _____.**

○ in the bowl

○ at a movie

○ in the attic

2 **The _____ is full of apples.**

○ tall tree

○ blue sea

○ big building

3 **When I am thirsty, I _____.**

○ chop wood

○ sing songs

○ drink water

4 **We had cake at my birthday _____.**

○ hike

○ party

○ flower

5 **Be _____ not to touch the oven.**

○ careful

○ happy

○ silly

Name: _____

Test-Taking Practice: Grade K

Directions: Listen to the story. Then fill in the circle next to the picture that best answers the question.

Wendy was Tanya's baby sister. Wendy wanted to do everything Tanya did. Tanya was going to eat the last piece of cake. Wendy wanted a piece too. Tanya got an idea. She cut the piece of cake in half. They ate their snack together.

1   Which picture shows Wendy?

○   ○   ○

2   What did Wendy want to eat?

○   ○   ○

Test-Taking Practice: Grade K

Directions: Look at the picture in each box. Fill in the circle next to each beginning sound.

○**p** ○**t**	○**b** ○**p**	○**n** ○**c**
○**n** ○**b**	○**t** ○**n**	○**t** ○**b**
○**p** ○**b**	○**c** ○**p**	○**c** ○**b**

Name: _____

Test-Taking Practice: Grade K

Directions: Look at the picture in each box. Fill in the circle next to each ending sound.

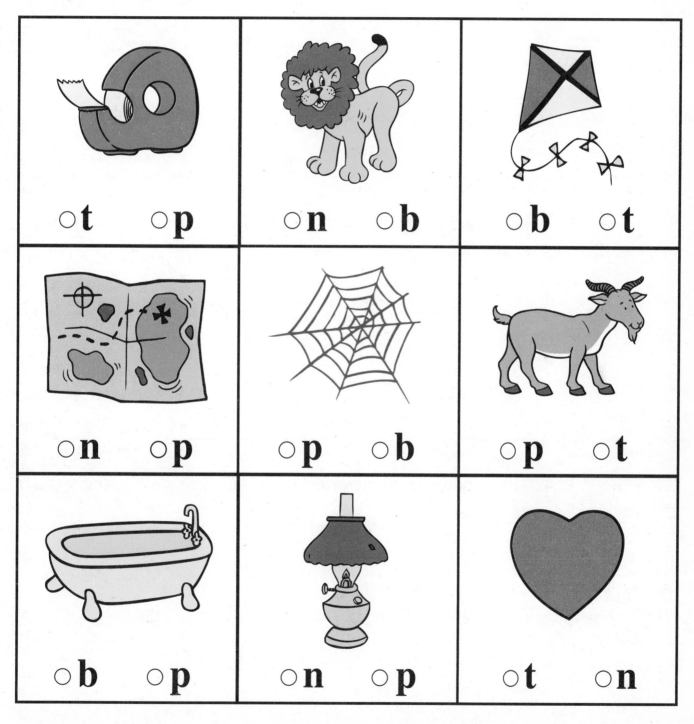

Name: _____

Test-Taking Practice: Grade K

Directions: Listen to an adult say the word. Fill in the circle next to the word that has the same beginning sound.

1 desk

   ○ chair   ○ bat   ○ den

Directions: Listen to an adult say the word. Fill in the circle next to the word that has the same ending sound.

2 make

   ○ man   ○ nose   ○ rock

Directions: Listen to an adult say the word. Fill in the circle next to the word that rhymes.

3 find

   ○ left   ○ fun   ○ kind

Name: _____

Test-Taking Practice: Grade K

Directions: Listen for the word that has the same beginning sound as <u>street</u>. Fill in the circle next to that word.

1   strong   teeth   horse
        ○   ○   ○

Directions: Listen for the word that has the same beginning sound as <u>flat</u>. Fill in the circle next to that word.

2   tall   sat   fly
        ○   ○   ○

Directions: Listen for the word that has the same middle sound as <u>ride</u>. Fill in the circle next to that word.

3   miss   line   hair
        ○   ○   ○

Directions: Listen for the word that has the same middle sound as <u>get</u>. Fill in the circle next to that word.

4   ten   here   real
        ○   ○   ○

Name: _____

Test-Taking Practice: Grade K

Directions: Listen for the word that has the same beginning sound as <u>large</u>. Fill in the circle next to that word.

1

         leaf   arm   hill

         ○   ○   ○

Directions: Listen for the word that has the same beginning sound as <u>golf</u>. Fill in the circle next to that word.

2

         fox   tall   gone

         ○   ○   ○

Directions: Listen for the word that has the same middle sound as <u>hat</u>. Fill in the circle next to that word.

3   bag   buy   bit

        ○   ○   ○

Directions: Listen for the word that has the same middle sound as <u>wet</u>. Fill in the circle next to that word.

4   room   rest   roll

        ○   ○   ○

Test-Taking Practice: Grade 1

Directions: Listen to the story and fill in the circle for the answer to each question. Carol wanted to ride her bike with her friend, Ramon. They would ride up the street to the playground. When she went to get her bike, Carol saw it had a flat tire.

1   **Which picture shows what was wrong with Carol's bike?**

   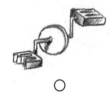

○   ○   ○

2   **Find the picture that shows where Ramon and Carol wanted to go.**

○   ○   ○

3   **Find the sentence that tells how Carol probably felt when she saw her bike.**

She was happy.   She was sad.   She didn't care.

○   ○   ○

Listen to the rest of the story: Carol told her big brother about the tire. He said he could fix it right away. He fixed the tire, and Carol could ride with her friend.

4   **Mark the circle under the words that tell what this story was mostly about.**

going for a ride   fixing a bike   going to the playground

○   ○   ○

Name: _____

Test-Taking Practice: Grade 1

Directions: Find the word that means <u>big</u>. Fill in the circle next to that word.

  SAMPLE A

funny	cool	large	empty
○	○	○	○

Think about the definition.
Choose the best answer.

1 **Find the word that means twelve months.**

yard	year	pail	mile
○	○	○	○

2 **Find the word that means a kind of fruit.**

tree	bread	milk	orange
○	○	○	○

3 **Find the word that means a place where people live.**

house	chair	roof	tree
○	○	○	○

4 **Find the word that means something made of wood.**

dress	glove	brick	log
○	○	○	○

5 **Find the word that means something that makes honey.**

fish	bird	bee	cow
○	○	○	○

Test-Taking Practice: Grade 1

Directions: Find the word that means something that you read. Fill in the circle next to that word.

SAMPLE A

snack	book	seat	sound
○	○	○	○

1 **Which word means a small city?**

road	hill	house	town
○	○	○	○

2 **Which word means a body of water?**

lake	field	tree	cave
○	○	○	○

Directions: Find the word that means about the same as the underlined word.

3 search for

- ○ race
- ○ jump
- ○ look
- ○ write

4 large boat

- ○ wagon
- ○ balloon
- ○ cart
- ○ ship

5 will listen

- ○ hear
- ○ taste
- ○ find
- ○ sell

6 wet cloth

- ○ damp
- ○ small
- ○ soft
- ○ warm

Test-Taking Practice: Grade 1

Directions: Which answer choice fits best in the blank? Fill in the circle next to that choice.

 SAMPLE A   The _____ deer was shy. It stood beside its mother.

   ○ young   ○ brave

   ○ fast   ○ tall

 **TIPS**   Try each answer in the blank.

Directions: For numbers 1–6, find the word that best fits in the blank.

1 We must _____ soon or we will be late.

   ○ play   ○ start

   ○ call   ○ study

2 Put the ladder _____ the wall so I can climb up.

   ○ inside   ○ along

   ○ against   ○ below

3 Put the food on the _____ and then serve it.

   ○ dishes   ○ floor

   ○ stove   ○ chairs

4 The _____ was bright. It was easy to see even though it was night.

   ○ moon   ○ cloud

   ○ sun   ○ fog

5 Helena _____ her room blue and white.

   ○ cleaned   ○ fixed

   ○ slept   ○ painted

6 The cat's claws are _____ , so be careful when you play with it.

   ○ soft   ○ sharp

   ○ furry   ○ nice

Name: _____

Test-Taking Practice: Grade 1

Directions: Which answer choice fits best in the blank? Fill in the circle next to that choice.

SAMPLE A The ice was so _____ . We couldn't walk on it.

safe ○   thin ○   thick ○   cold ○

1 The box was so heavy it took two of us to _____ it.

lift ○   see ○   find ○

2 The oven is hot. Now we can _____ the cookies.

taste ○   eat ○   buy ○   bake ○

3 Put your coat in the _____ and then close the door.

garden ○   box ○   closet ○

4 Each week, I try to save some money in my _____ .

pocket ○   wallet ○   bank ○

5 The _____ at the beach were pretty. I took some home.

shells ○   water ○   crowd ○

Name: _____

Test-Taking Practice: Grade 1

Directions: Find the word that has the same beginning sound as <u>joke</u>. Fill in the circle next to that word.

SAMPLE A

pay	jump	mop	funny
○	○	○	○

1 Which word has the same beginning sound as <u>pork</u>?

dust	late	pool	clap
○	○	○	○

2 Which word has the same beginning sound as <u>van</u>?

toast	move	near	vote
○	○	○	○

3 Which word has the same beginning sound as <u>chest</u>?

choose	touch	song	these
○	○	○	○

4 Which word has the same ending sound as <u>knob</u>?

coat	lunch	dear	club
○	○	○	○

5 Which word has the same ending sound as <u>stew</u>?

net	wheel	now	give
○	○	○	○

6 Which word has the same ending sound as <u>third</u>?

hard	land	barn	dark
○	○	○	○

Name: _____

Test-Taking Practice: Grade 1

Directions: Which word has the same ending sound as <u>far</u>? Fill in the circle next to that word.

SAMPLE A

fun	off	ran	her
○	○	○	○

Say each answer to yourself.
Listen for the ending sound.

1 Which word has the same ending sound as <u>pin</u>?

trap	can	nose	pet
○	○	○	○

2 Which word has the same ending sound as <u>hit</u>?

not	hear	win	dish
○	○	○	○

3 Which word has the same ending sound as <u>have</u>?

wish	head	van	love
○	○	○	○

4 Which word has the same ending sound as <u>want</u>?

wind	sent	both
○	○	○

5 Which word has the same ending sound as <u>dirt</u>?

learn	bird	heart
○	○	○

Test-Taking Practice: Grade 1

Directions: Which word has the same middle sound as <u>bird</u>? Fill in the circle next to that word.

SAMPLE
A

like	heard	noise	miss
○	○	○	○

1 Find the word that has the same middle sound as <u>cow</u>.

hope	roar	round	pop
○	○	○	○

2 Find the word that has the same middle sound as <u>tent</u>.

rest	team	seem	they
○	○	○	○

3 Find the word that has the same middle sound as <u>rain</u>.

load	that	bread	game
○	○	○	○

4 Find the word that has the same middle sound as <u>fruit</u>.

root	hope	boat	cow
○	○	○	○

5 Find the word that has the same middle sound as <u>kite</u>.

fair	list	have	five
○	○	○	○

Test-Taking Practice: Grade 2

1 **Find the picture of what probably happened first.**

    ○   ○

Directions: Find the sentence that best fits in the blank. Fill in its circle.

2 **Mr. Jennings went shopping. He bought food for dinner.**

_____.

- ○ Then he came home.
- ○ Then he stayed at the store.
- ○ Then he sold the food.

---

3 **The kitten is hungry. Lettie knows what to do.**

_____.

- ○ The kitten runs away.
- ○ She gives it a bath.
- ○ She feeds the kitten.

Test-Taking Practice: Grade 2

Up and Away

I fasten my belt
And close my eyes;
The next time I look
We're up in the skies!

My very first chance
To soar like a bird
We're flying so high
I can't say a word.

Blue sky above;
White clouds below;
In a window seat
I enjoy the show.

Then the plane lands
And I head for the door.
I'm going to ask Mom
When I can fly more.

Directions: Fill in the circle next to the answer for each of these questions.

1 **What does the child do first?**

fix belt ○

eat food ○

read book ○

2 **Where must the child be sitting?**

○

○

○

Test-Taking Practice: Grade 2

3 If the child added a sentence to the poem about traveling with a relative, it might be

> Beside me sat
> _____ .

My best friend, Nat.
○

My sister, Pat.
○

A man with a hat.
○

---

4 The child in the poem says

> To soar like a bird.

To soar like a bird is to

step.
○

land.
○

fly.
○

---

5 The child in the poem says

> The next time I look
> We're up in the skies!

What does the child mean?

○   The plane rose quickly.

○   She saw the plane fly.

○   The plane is landing.

Test-Taking Practice: Grade 2

6   **In the poem, what is soaring?**

      train   plane   car

       ○   ○   ○

---

7   In this poem, the child <u>fastens</u> a belt. **What is the <u>opposite</u> of <u>fasten</u>?**

    tighten   unfasten   attach   move

     ○   ○   ○   ○

Directions: Find the sentence that best fits in the blank. Fill in its circle.

8   People need clothes when they travel. _____.
      The suitcase is stored in the plane.

    ○   Planes are faster than cars.

    ○   An airport is a large building.

    ○   They put clothes in a suitcase.

---

9   An airport is a busy place. _____.
      Planes take off and land all day.

    ○   You drive to get to the airport.

    ○   Many people come and go.

    ○   Sometimes a plane ride is long.

Test-Taking Practice: Grade 2

Directions: Fill in the circle next to each answer.

1   Kyle <u>actually</u> knew Sign Language.

Which of these words means the same as <u>actually</u>?

rarely   really   seldom
  ○   ○   ○

---

2   Patsy said she was <u>nervous</u>.

Which of these words means the <u>opposite</u> of <u>nervous</u>?

calm   annoyed   frightened
  ○   ○   ○

---

3   **Find the word that has the same vowel, or middle, sound as <u>found</u>.**

road   flood   clown
  ○   ○   ○

---

4   **Which of these is the root, or base, word of <u>trying</u>?**

try   ing   ryin
  ○   ○   ○

> * A base word is a word from which other words are made.

---

5   **Which of these is the root, or base, word of <u>reached</u>?**

each   ched   reach
  ○   ○   ○

Test-Taking Practice: Grade 2

Directions: Which word fits best in the blank? Fill in the circle next to that choice.

SAMPLE A　　**The boat began to _____ .**

climb　　　　wait　　　　sink　　　　talk
○　　　　○　　　　○　　　　○

Directions: For numbers 1 and 2, find the words that best complete the story. Fill in the circle next to that choice.

The __(1)__ was easy to enter. All you had to do was show up at the park. To win, you had to __(2)__ how many jelly beans were in a jar.

1 ○ door　○ tunnel　　**2** ○ play　○ guess
　○ contest　○ room　　　　○ read　○ count

Directions: For Sample B and numbers 3 and 4, which word fits best in both blanks? Fill in the circle next to that choice.

SAMPLE B　　**It was a _____ day. The speeder paid a _____ .**

nice　　　　fine　　　　ticket　　　　great
○　　　　○　　　　○　　　　○

3　_____ the light over here.　　**4**　**The puppy began to _____ .**
　The _____ on this pencil broke.　　**The car needs a new _____ .**

○ point　○ shine　　　○ sleep　○ light
○ eraser　○ top　　　　○ run　○ tire

TIPS　Use the meaning of the sentence to find the answer.

Test-Taking Practice: Grade 2

SAMPLE A

Directions: Find the word that has the same ending sound as <u>camp</u>. Fill in its circle.

dump	trip	dirt
○	○	○

SAMPLE B

Directions: Find the word that is a compound word, a word that is made up of two smaller words. Fill in its circle.

building	darkness	plumbing	sidewalk
○	○	○	○

1 **Find the word that has the same ending sound as <u>best</u>.**

loss	salt	most
○	○	○

2 **Find the word that has the same vowel sound as <u>same</u>.**

ham	rain	soar	sand
○	○	○	○

3 **What does the word <u>aren't</u> mean?**

are not	are late	are most	are then
○	○	○	○

4 **Find the word that is a compound word.**

footprint	remember	narrow	explain
○	○	○	○

5 **What is the root word of <u>kindness</u>?**

in	ness	kind	ind
○	○	○	○

6 **What is suffix of <u>careful</u>?**

are	car	reful	ful
○	○	○	○

Test-Taking Practice: Grade 2

Directions: Fill in the circle next to the word that is spelled correctly.

 SAMPLE A   **Did you _____ who was there?**

notise	notice	notisce	notis
○	○	○	○

1   **Our _____ run is about two miles.**

dailly	dailey	daley	daily
○	○	○	○

2   **The _____ is open.**

wendow	windo	window	windowe
○	○	○	○

Directions: Fill in the circle next to the word that is not spelled correctly. If all of the words are spelled correctly, choose "All correct."

SAMPLE B
- ○ look <u>around</u>
- ○ <u>hidden</u> prize
- ○ <u>never</u> mind
- ○ All correct

4
- ○ <u>floating</u> log
- ○ <u>windy</u> day
- ○ <u>many</u> birds
- ○ All correct

5
- ○ hot <u>paivment</u>
- ○ strong <u>branch</u>
- ○ <u>right</u> answer
- ○ All correct

Test-Taking Practice Answer Key: Grade K

Page 279
   1. tasty
   2. under
   3. rice
   4. winner

Page 280
   1. in the bowl
   2. tall tree
   3. drink water
   4. party
   5. careful

Page 281
   1. the second picture
   2. Wendy wanted to eat cake.

Page 282

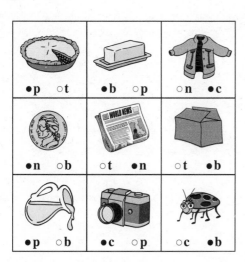

Page 283

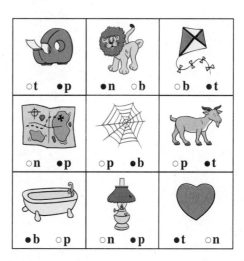

Page 284
   1. den
   2. rock
   3. kind

Page 285
   5. strong
   6. fly
   7. line
   8. ten

Page 286
   7. leaf
   8. gone
   9. bag
   10. rest

Test-Taking Practice Answer Key: Grade 1

Page 287
1. the third picture
2. the first picture
3. She was sad.
4. fixing a bike

Page 288
A. large
1. year
2. orange
3. house
4. log
5. bee

Page 289
A. book
1. town
2. lake
3. look
4. ship
5. hear
6. damp

Page 290
A. young
1. start
2. against
3. dishes
4. moon
5. painted
6. sharp

Page 291
A. thin
1. lift
2. bake
3. closet
4. bank
5. shells

Page 292
A. jump
1. pool
2. vote
3. choose
4. club
5. now
6. hard

Page 293
A. her
1. can
2. not
3. love
4. sent
5. heart

Page 294
A. heard
1. round
2. rest
3. game
4. root
5. five

Test-Taking Practice Answer Key: Grade 2

Page 295
1. first picture
2. Then he came home.
3. She feeds the kitten.

Page 296
1. fix belt
2. second picture

Page 297
3. My sister, Pat
4. fly
5. The plane rose quickly.

Page 298
6. plane
7. unfasten
8. They put clothes in a suitcase.
9. Many people come and go.

Page 299
1. really
2. calm
3. clown
4. try
5. reach

Page 300
A. sink
1. contest
2. guess
B. fine
3. point
4. tire

Page 301
A. dump
B. sidewalk
1. most
2. rain
3. are not
4. footprint
5. kind
6. ful

Page 302
A. notice
1. daily
2. window
B. All correct
4. All correct
5. hot paivment

ANSWER KEY

To remove this Answer Key pull along perforation

PHONICS

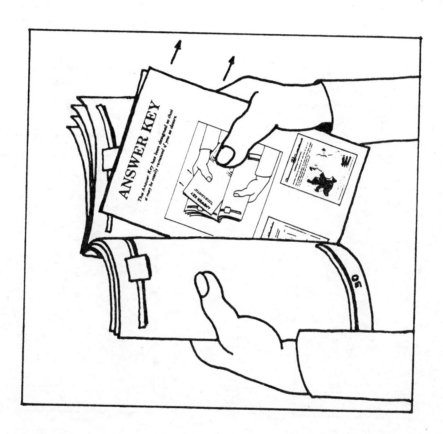

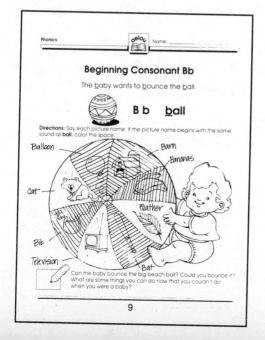

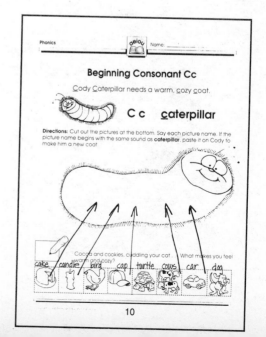

Beginning Consonant Tt

Tommy put too many toys in the tub.

T t   tub

Directions: Say the picture name for each toy in the tub. If the picture name begins with the same sound as **tub**, mark an X on it.

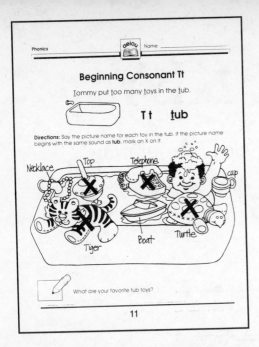

Necklace Top Telephone cup
Tiger Boat Turtle

What are your favorite tub toys?

11

Review Beginning Consonants

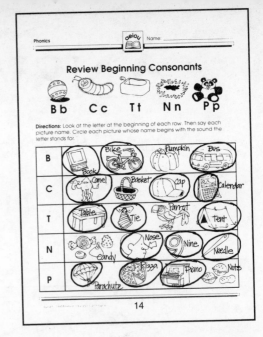

B b   C c   T t   N n   P p

Directions: Look at the letter at the beginning of each row. Then say each picture name. Circle each picture whose name begins with the sound the letter stands for.

B	Book	Bike	Pumpkin	Bus
C	Camel	Basket	Cap	Calendar
T	Table	Tie	Parrot	Tent
N	Candy	Nose	Nine	Needle
P	Parachute	Pizza	Piano	Nuts

14

Beginning Consonant Nn

The sleepy baby birds want to nap in their nest.

N n   nest

Directions: Help the birds find their nest. Follow the path with the pictures whose names begin with the same sound as **nest**.

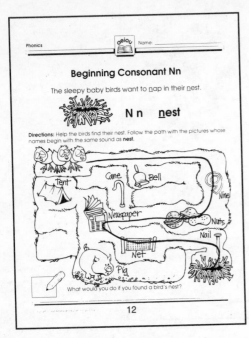

Tent Cane Bell Nine
Newspaper Nuts Nail
Net Pig

What would you do if you found a bird's nest?

12

Review Beginning Consonants

Directions: Say each picture name. Circle the letter that stands for the beginning sound.

Pie — P T	Butter — B P	Coat — N C	Tire — B T
Nickel — N B	Newspaper — T N	Box — T B	Two — T P
Pitcher — P B	Camera — C P	Bug — C B	Cape — T C
Tomato — T P	Nurse — N C	Pail — N P	Pear — B P
Bed — B C	Numbers — P N	Cookies — C B	Turkey — C T

15

Beginning Consonant Pp

Pam packs her panda for a sleepover.

P p   panda

Directions: Pam only packs things whose names begin with the same sound as **panda**. What else will she pack? Say the picture names. Draw a line from Pam to each picture whose name begins with the same sound as **Pam** and **panda**.

Toothbrush Necklace Pajamas
Pillow comb Pencil
Pam Purse Pin Belt

Make a list of things you need for a sleepover. Use your list the next time you pack.

13

Ending Consonants

Directions: Say each picture name. Fill in the circle next to the letter that stands for the **last** sound.

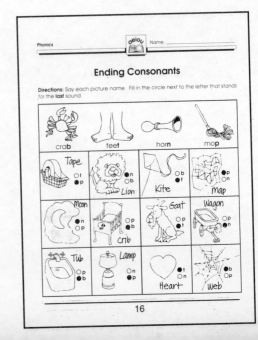

crab   feet   horn   mop

Tape — t p	Lion — n b	Kite — b t	map — p n
Moon — n p	crib — b b	Goat — p t	Wagon — p n
Tub — b t	Lamp — n p	Heart — t n	Web — b p

16

308

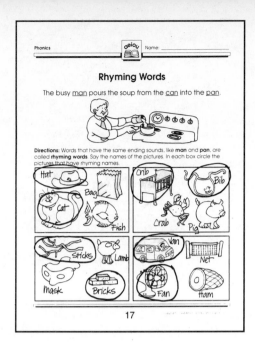

Rhyming Words

The busy <u>man</u> pours the soup from the <u>can</u> into the <u>pan</u>.

Directions: Words that have the same ending sounds, like **man** and **pan**, are called **rhyming words**. Say the names of the pictures. In each box circle the pictures that have rhyming names.

17

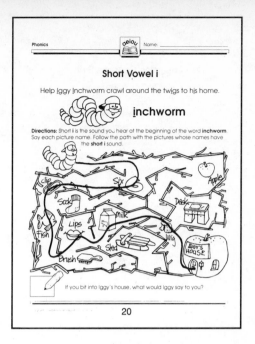

Short Vowel i

Help Iggy Inchworm crawl around the twigs to his home.

inchworm

Directions: Short **i** is the sound you hear at the beginning of the word **inchworm**. Say each picture name. Follow the path with the pictures whose names have the **short i** sound.

If you bit into Iggy's house, what would Iggy say to you?

20

Short Vowel a

The band of ants play rat-a-tat-tat!

ants

Directions: Short **a** is the sound you hear at the beginning of the word **ants**. Only animals whose names have the **short a** sound can play in the ants' band. Say each picture name. Circle the picture if you hear the **short a** sound.

If the animal band marched past your house, what would you do?

18

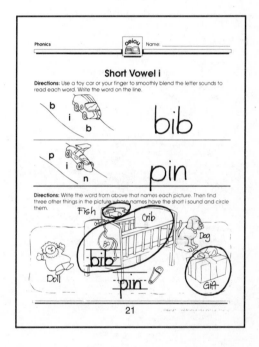

Short Vowel i

Directions: Use a toy car or your finger to smoothly blend the letter sounds to read each word. Write the word on the line.

bib

pin

Directions: Write the word from above that names each picture. Then find three other things in the picture whose names have the short i sound and circle them.

21

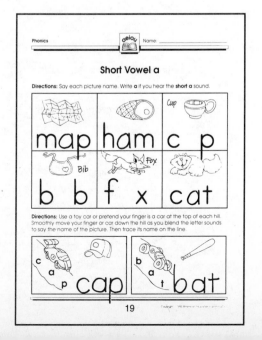

Short Vowel a

Directions: Say each picture name. Write **a** if you hear the **short a** sound.

map   ham   c p

b   b f x   cat

Directions: Use a toy car or pretend your finger is a car at the top of each hill. Smoothly move your finger or car down the hill as you blend the letter sounds to say the name of the picture. Then trace its name on the line.

cap   bat

19

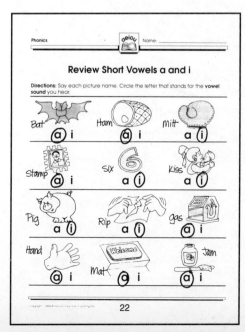

Review Short Vowels a and i

Directions: Say each picture name. Circle the letter that stands for the **vowel sound** you hear.

22

309

Beginning Consonant Hh

Raise your <u>h</u>and and wave <u>h</u>ello!

H h   <u>h</u>and

Directions: Say each picture name. If the picture name begins with the same sound as **hand**, color the bead.

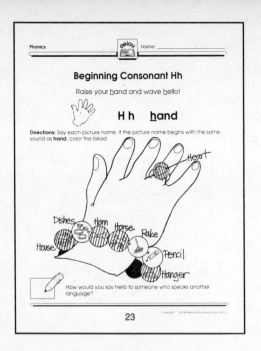

How would you say hello to someone who speaks another language?

23

Beginning Consonant Ff

Where do these <u>f</u>ussy <u>f</u>ireflies land?

F f   <u>f</u>ireflies

Directions: These fussy fireflies only land on things whose names begin with the same sound as **fireflies**. Cut out the pictures at the bottom. Paste them on things in the picture whose names begin with the same sound as **fireflies**.

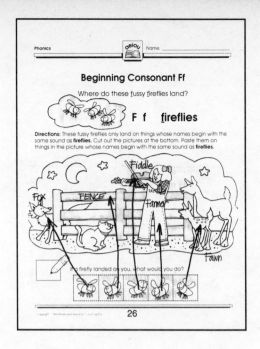

If a firefly landed on you, what would you do?

26

Beginning Consonant Dd

Oh, no! A <u>d</u>inosaur is at the <u>d</u>oor!

D d   <u>d</u>inosaur

Directions: Say the picture names in each box on the door. Circle the picture whose name begins with the same sound as **dinosaur**.

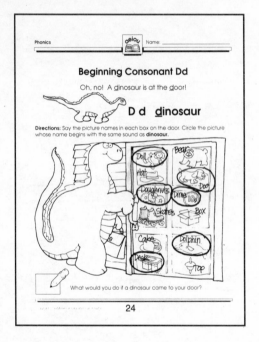

What would you do if a dinosaur came to your door?

24

Beginning Consonant Gg

What do you see when you wear goofy goggles?

G g   goggles

Directions: Say each picture name. If the picture name begins with the same sound as **goggles**, circle it.

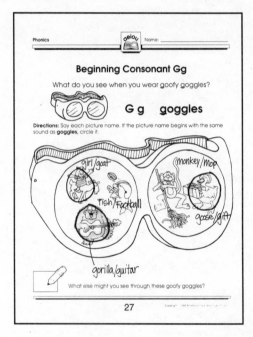

What else might you see through these goofy goggles?

27

Beginning Consonant Rr

The <u>r</u>accoon <u>r</u>uns in the <u>r</u>ain.

R r   <u>r</u>accoon

Directions: Say each picture name. Color the space if the picture name begins with the same sound as **raccoon**.

Who does the raccoon visit to get out of the rain?

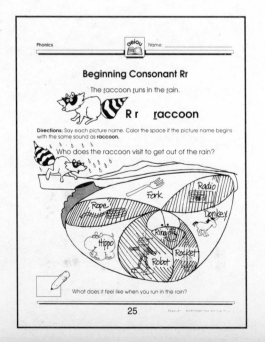

What does it feel like when you run in the rain?

25

Beginning Consonant Mm

<u>M</u>acaroni and <u>m</u>eatballs make <u>M</u>ike <u>m</u>essy!

M m   <u>m</u>acaroni <u>m</u>eatballs

Directions: Say each picture name. If the picture name begins with the same sound as **macaroni** and **meatballs**, color the meatball.

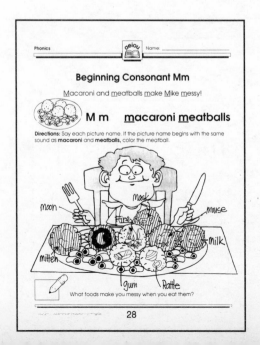

What foods make you messy when you eat them?

28

310

Review Beginning Consonants

H h	D d	R r
F f	G g	M m

Directions: Look at the letter in each box. Then say each picture name. Circle the picture whose name begins with the sound the letter stands for.

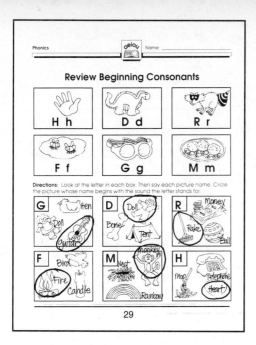

29

Short Vowel o

This octopus wants socks.

octopus

Directions: Short **o** is the sound you hear at the beginning of the word **octopus**. Say each picture name. Color the sock if you hear the **short o** sound. Does this octopus have enough colored socks?

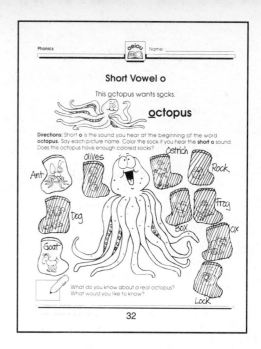

What do you know about a real octopus?
What would you like to know?

32

Review Beginning Consonants

Directions: Say each picture name. Listen to the beginning sound. Find the letter that stands for the sound on a crayon. Use your crayons to make each mitten the right color.

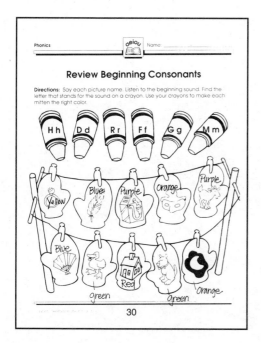

30

Short Vowel o

Directions: Say each picture name. Write **o** if you hear the **short o** sound.

cot	p_n	dog
h_t	box	rod

Directions: Use a toy car or pretend your finger is a car at the top of each hill. Smoothly move your finger or car down the hill as you blend the letter sounds to say the name of the picture. Then trace its name on the line.

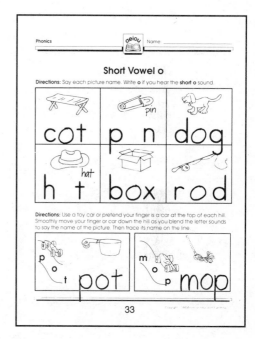

33

Ending Consonants

be**d**   ba**g**   ja**m**

Directions: Write the missing letter to complete each word.

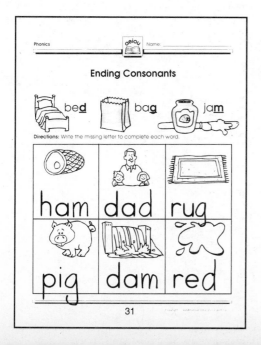

ham	dad	rug
pig	dam	red

31

Short Vowel u

Decorate the big beach umbrella.

umbrella

Directions: Short **u** is the sound you hear at the beginning of the word **umbrella**. Cut out the pictures at the bottom of the page. Say each picture name. If you hear the **short u** sound, paste the picture on the umbrella.

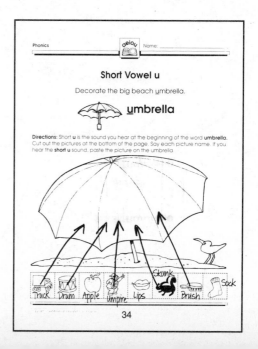

34

311

Short Vowel u

Directions: Use a toy car or your finger to smoothly blend the letter sounds to read each word. Then write it on the line.

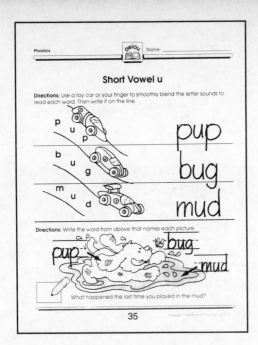

p u p — pup
b u g — bug
m u d — mud

Directions: Write the word from above that names each picture.

pup   bug   mud

What happened the last time you played in the mud?

35

Review Short Vowels o, u, e

Directions: Say each picture name. Circle the letter that stands for the vowel sound you hear.

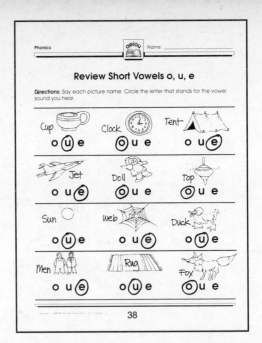

Cup — o (u) e	Clock — (o) u e	Tent — o u (e)
Jet — o u (e)	Doll — (o) u e	Top — (o) u e
Sun — o (u) e	Web — o u (e)	Duck — o (u) e
Men — o u (e)	Rug — o (u) e	Fox — (o) u e

38

Short Vowel e

Help the red hen find her eggs.

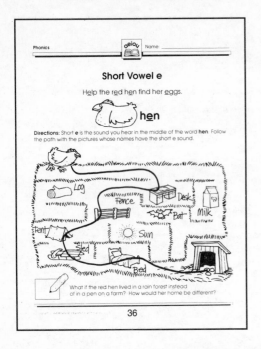

hen

Directions: Short **e** is the sound you hear in the middle of the word **hen**. Follow the path with the pictures whose names have the short e sound.

Log   Desk   Milk   Fence   Bat   Tent   Sun   Sled   Bed

What if the red hen lived in a rain forest instead of in a pen on a farm? How would her home be different?

36

Rhyming Words

Directions: Words that have the same ending sounds are called **rhyming words**. Say the names of the pictures. In each row, circle the picture that has the same ending sound as the first picture.

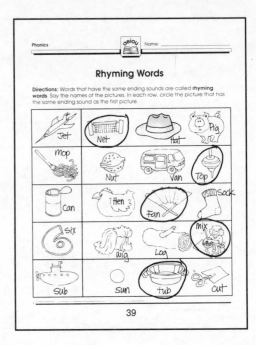

Jet	Net	Hat	Pig
Mop	Nut	Van	Top
Can	Hen	Fan	Sock
Six	Wig	Log	Mix
Sub	Sun	Tub	Cut

39

Short Vowel e

Directions: Use a toy car or your finger to smoothly blend the letter sounds to read each word. Write the word on the line. Then write the word that names each picture at the bottom.

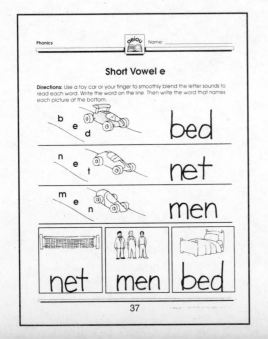

b e d — bed
n e t — net
m e n — men

net   men   bed

37

Sound Pattern -at

Pat wears her favorite hat to the costume party.

hat

Directions: Cut out the hat and feather. Cut on the dotted lines to make slits. Slip the feather through the hat. Slide the feather and read each new word.

Diagram

_____ at

40

312

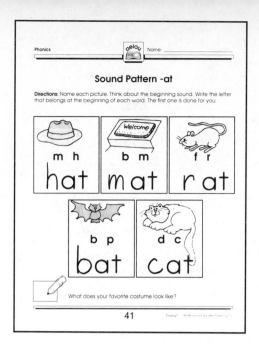

Sound Pattern -at

Directions: Name each picture. Think about the beginning sound. Write the letter that belongs at the beginning of each word. The first one is done for you.

m h — hat
b m — mat
f r — rat

b p — bat
d c — cat

What does your favorite costume look like?

41

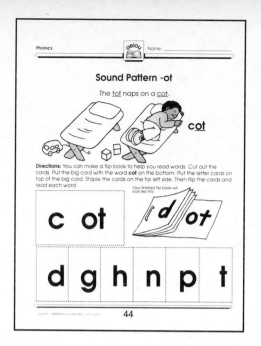

Sound Pattern -ot

The <u>tot</u> naps on a <u>cot</u>.

cot

Directions: You can make a flip book to help you read words. Cut out the cards. Put the big card with the word **cot** on the bottom. Put the letter cards on top of the big card. Staple the cards on the far left side. Then flip the cards and read each word.

Your finished flip book will look like this.

c ot   d ot

d g h n p t

44

Sound Pattern -in

Put used paper in the recycling <u>bin</u>. Help save our earth!

bin

Directions: Cut out the bin and paper. Cut on the dotted lines to make slits. Slip the paper through the slits on the bin. Slide the paper and read each new word.
Diagram:

b
p in

_ _ _ _ in

b
f
p
t

42

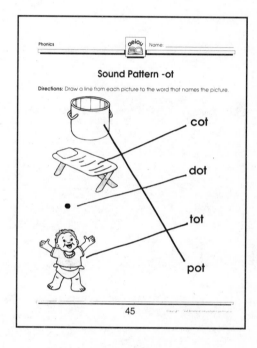

Sound Pattern -ot

Directions: Draw a line from each picture to the word that names the picture.

cot

dot

tot

pot

45

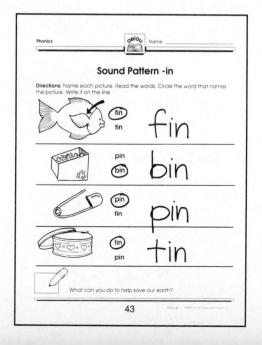

Sound Pattern -in

Directions: Name each picture. Read the words. Circle the word that names the picture. Write it on the line.

fin / tin — fin
pin / bin — bin
pin / fin — pin
tin / pin — tin

What can you do to help save our earth?

43

313

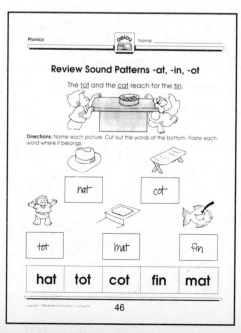

Review Sound Patterns -at, -in, -ot

The <u>tot</u> and the <u>cat</u> reach for the <u>tin</u>.

Directions: Name each picture. Cut out the words at the bottom. Paste each word where it belongs.

hat   cot

tot   mat   fin

hat tot cot fin mat

46

Review Sound Patterns -at, -in, -ot

c**at**   p**ot**   b**in**

Directions: Read each word at the top of the page. Look at the pictures below. Find a rhyming word that belongs with each picture. Write the rhyming word on the line.

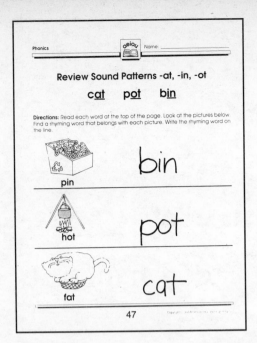

pin   bin

hot   pot

fat   cat

47

Sound Pattern -en

Ken has ten crayons.

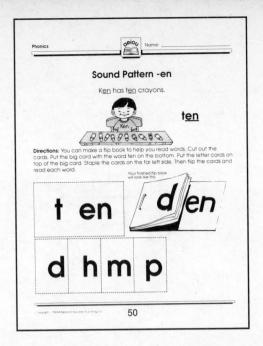

ten

Directions: You can make a flip book to help you read words. Cut out the cards. Put the big card with the word ten on the bottom. Put the letter cards on top of the big card. Staple the cards on the far left side. Then flip the cards and read each word.

Your finished flip book will look like this.

t en   d en

d h m p

50

Sound Pattern -ug

Can you find the b**ug** in this r**ug**?

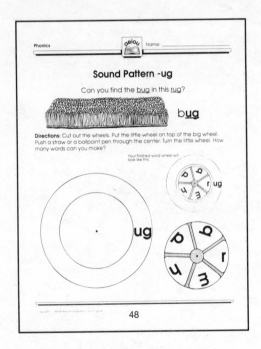

b**ug**

Directions: Cut out the wheels. Put the little wheel on top of the big wheel. Push a straw or a ballpoint pen through the center. Turn the little wheel. How many words can you make?

Your finished word wheel will look like this.

ug

48

Sound Pattern -en

Directions: Read or ask someone to help you read the rhyme. Circle the word that completes each line. Then write the word on the line.

(hen)   den
"I can't find my eggs!" said the little red   **hen** .

pen   (men)
She ran by some   **men** .

(ten)   hen
She ran by a big   **ten** .

men   (pen)
"My, what a surprise. They're right here in my   **pen** !"

51

Sound Pattern -ug

Directions: Read each sentence. The pictures will help you. Circle the word that completes the sentence. Then write it on the line.

(dug)   tug
Pup   **dug**   in the mud.

bug   (rug)
Pup stops on the   **rug** .

(hug)   mug
Mom gives Pup a big   **hug** .

49

314

Review Sound Patterns -ug and -en

Directions: Name each picture. Read the question. Circle the word that answers the question. Then write the word.

Is it a (mug) or a rug?   **mug**

Is it (ten) or a tan?   **ten**

Is it a bug or a (tug)?   **tug**

Is it hen or a (hug)?   **hug**

Is it (pen) or a cot?   **pen**

52

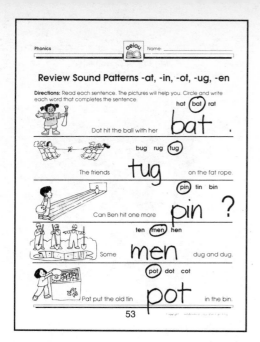

Review Sound Patterns -at, -in, -ot, -ug, -en

Directions: Read each sentence. The pictures will help you. Circle and write each word that completes the sentence.

hat (bat) rat

Dot hit the ball with her **bat** .

bug rug (tug)

The friends **tug** on the fat rope.

(pin) tin bin

Can Ben hit one more **pin** ?

ten (men) hen

Some **men** dug and dug.

(pot) dot cot

Pat put the old tin **pot** in the bin.

53

Review Sound Patterns -at, -in, -ot, -ug, -en

Directions: Read the sentences. Follow the path to help the tot find his cat.

1. Go over the mat.
2. Go under the cot.
3. Go around the pen.
4. Go past a bin.
5. Go around a tug.
6. Take the tot to his cat!

54

ABC Order
Directions: Draw a line to connect the dots. Follow the letters in ABC order.

55

abc Order
Directions: Draw a line to connect the dots. Follow the letters in abc order.

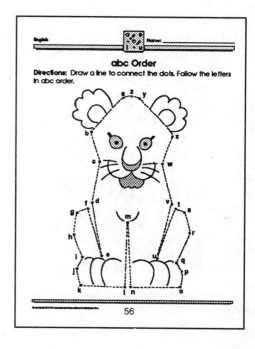

56

315

Matching Upper And Lower Case Letters
Directions: Draw a line from each upper case letter to its matching lower case letter.

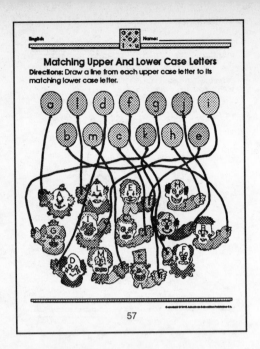

57

Writing Upper Case Letters
Directions: Trace each letter. Write each letter again next to the letter you traced.

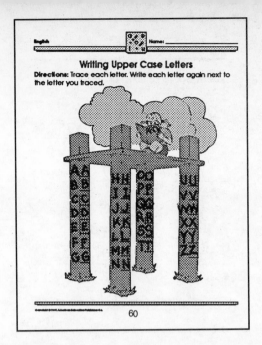

60

Matching Upper And Lower Case Letters
Directions: Draw a line from each upper case letter to its matching lower case letters.

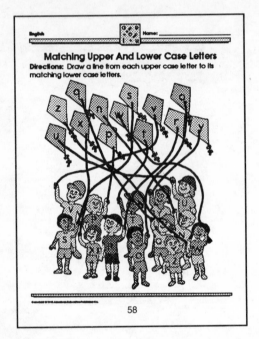

58

Writing Lower Case Letters
Directions: Trace each letter. Write each letter again next to the letter you traced.

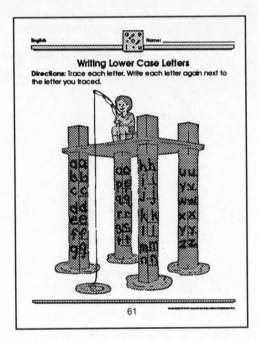

61

Discrimination Of a, b, d
Directions: Color the butterflies.
a = yellow, b = orange, d = purple

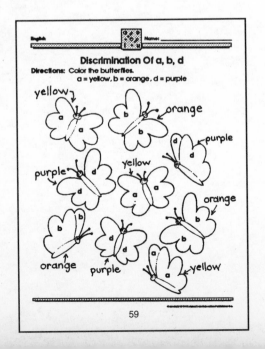

59

Review
Directions: Fill in the missing upper and lower case letters to complete the alphabet.

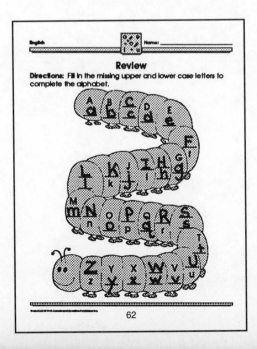

62

316

Beginning Consonant Sounds Bb, Cc, Dd

Directions: Say the sound that the letters Bb, Cc, Dd make. (Bb = buh, Cc = kuh, Dd = duh). Then say the name of each picture. If the first sound matches the letter, color it blue.

63

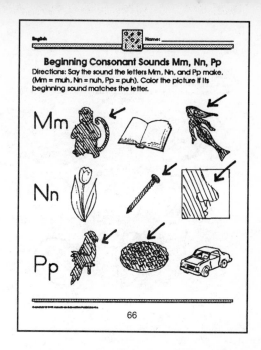

Beginning Consonant Sounds Mm, Nn, Pp

Directions: Say the sound the letters Mm, Nn, and Pp make. (Mm = muh, Nn = nuh, Pp = puh). Color the picture if its beginning sound matches the letter.

Mm

Nn

Pp

66

Beginning Consonant Sounds Ff, Gg, Hh

Directions: Say the sounds for the letters Ff, Gg, Hh. (Ff = fuh, Gg = guh, Hh = huh). Draw a circle around the picture if it begins with the letter in the column.

Ff   Gg   Hh

64

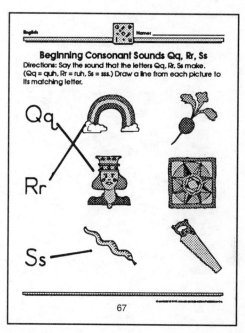

Beginning Consonant Sounds Qq, Rr, Ss

Directions: Say the sound that the letters Qq, Rr, Ss make. (Qq = quh, Rr = ruh, Ss = sss.) Draw a line from each picture to its matching letter.

Qq

Rr

Ss

67

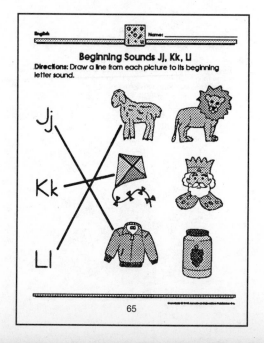

Beginning Sounds Jj, Kk, Ll

Directions: Draw a line from each picture to its beginning letter sound.

Jj

Kk

Ll

65

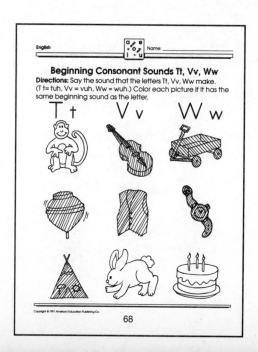

Beginning Consonant Sounds Tt, Vv, Ww

Directions: Say the sound that the letters Tt, Vv, Ww make. (T t= tuh, Vv = vuh, Ww = wuh.) Color each picture if it has the same beginning sound as the letter.

T t   V v   W w

68

317

Beginning Consonant Sounds Xx, Yy, Zz

Directions: Say the sound that the letters Xx, Yy, Zz make. (Xx = zuh, as in xray; Yy = yuh; Zz = zuh. Sometimes Xx says its own name, as in xray.) Draw a circle around each picture if its beginning sound matches the letter.

Xx

Yy

Zz

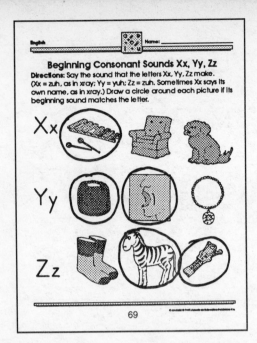

69

Beginning Short Vowel Sounds: Ee

Directions: Say the short vowel sound for the letter Ee. (It makes the same sound as the "e" in the word egg.) Look at the pictures. Color the pictures if they begin with the sound of the short vowel Ee.

Ee

color

color

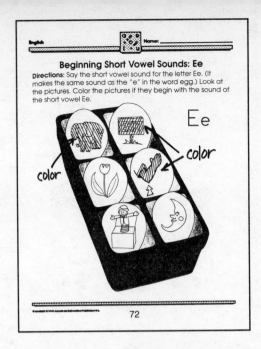

72

Review

Directions: Look at each picture. Say its name. Write the lower case letter for the beginning sound in each picture.

b   j   m   w

q   t   x   z

f   c   k   h

n   r   v   s

y   g   d   l   p

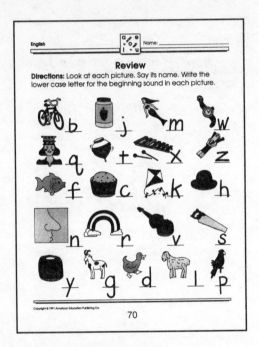

Copyright © 1991 American Education Publishing Co.

70

Beginning Short Vowel Sounds: Ii

Directions: Say the short vowel sound for the letter Ii. (The short vowel sound for the letter Ii sounds like the "I" in Indian.) Look at the pictures. Color the pictures that begin with the short vowel sound of Ii.

Ii

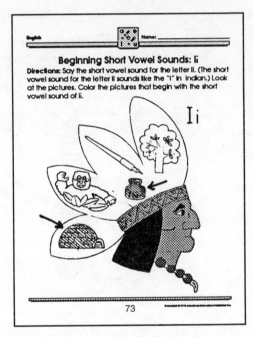

73

Beginning Short Vowel Sounds: A

Directions: Say the sound for the letter Aa. (The short vowel sound for Aa is heard at the beginning of the word alligator.) Color the pictures that begin with the short vowel sound.

Aa

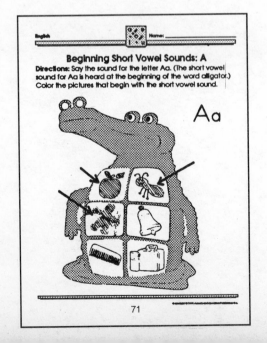

71

Beginning Short Vowel Sounds: Oo

Directions: Say the short vowel sound for Oo. (It makes the same sound as the "O" in Oscar.) Look at the pictures. Color the pictures that begin with the sound of Oo.

Oo

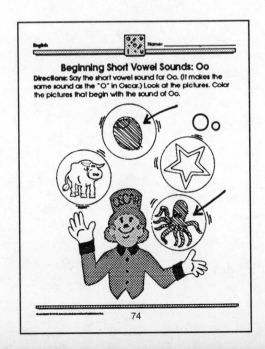

74

318

Beginning Short Vowel Sounds: Uu

Directions: 1) Say the sound for the letter Uu. (It makes the same sound as the "u" in umbrella.) 2) Look at the pictures and say each word. 3) Draw pictures of your uncle, something that goes up and an umbrella.

uncle

up

umbrella

Uu

pictures vary

75

Review

Directions: 1) Look at each picture and say its name. 2) Write the beginning or middle vowel sound that you hear. 3) If you hear the sound at the beginning of the word, color the picture blue. 4) If you hear the sound in the middle of the word, color the picture yellow.

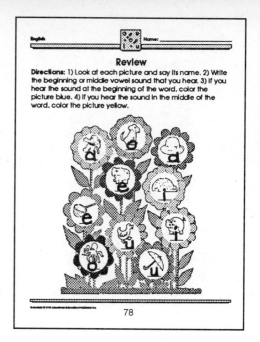

78

Middle Sounds With Short Vowels

Directions: Say the name of each picture. Listen for the middle sound. Draw a line between the picture and its matching letter.

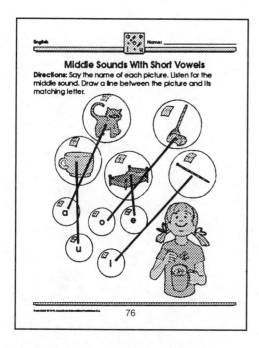

76

Words With Short Vowel Aa

Directions: Read the words. Draw a line from the picture to its matching word.

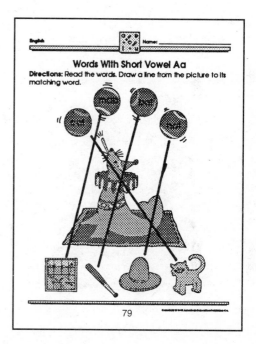

79

Middle Sounds: Short Vowel Sounds

Directions: Look at the pictures. Write the letter for the sound you hear in the middle of the word.

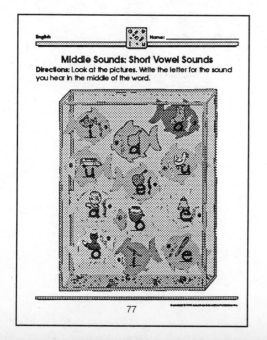

77

Words With Short Vowel Ee

Directions: Read the words. Circle the picture whose sound has short vowel e.

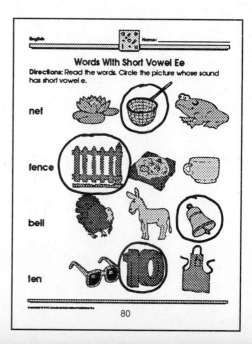

net

fence

bell

ten

80

319

Words With Short Vowel Ii

Directions: Read the words. Draw a line from each word to its matching picture.

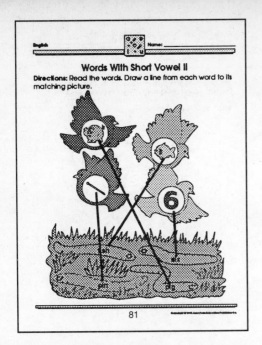

Words With Short Vowel Oo

Directions: Look at the pictures and read the words. Draw a line from each picture to the word that describes it.

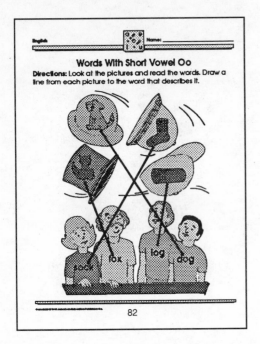

sock   fox   log   dog

Words With Short Vowel Uu

Directions: Look at the pictures and read the words. Draw a line between each picture and the word that describes it.

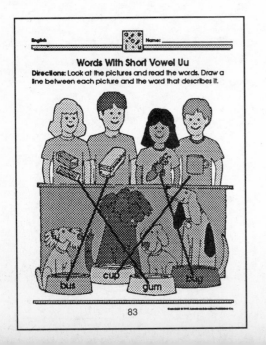

bus   cup   gum

Review

Directions: Look at the pictures and read the words. Draw a line between each picture and the word that describes it.

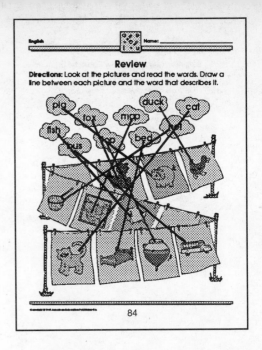

pig   fox   duck   cat
fish   map   bed
bus

Which Are Opposites?

Directions: Draw a line between the opposites.

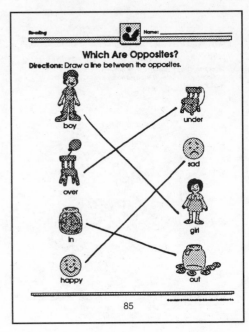

boy   under
over   sad
in   girl
happy   out

What Belongs?

Directions: Color the pictures in each row that belong together. Draw an X through the one that does not belong.

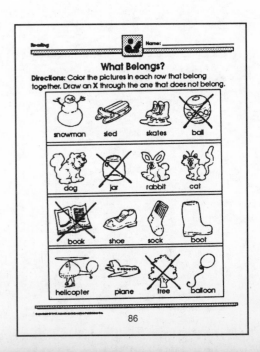

snowman	sled	skates	ball
dog	jar	rabbit	cat
book	shoe	sock	boot
helicopter	plane	tree	balloon

320

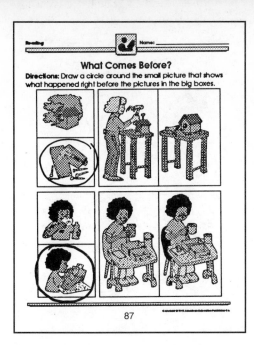

What Comes Before?

Directions: Draw a circle around the small picture that shows what happened right before the pictures in the big boxes.

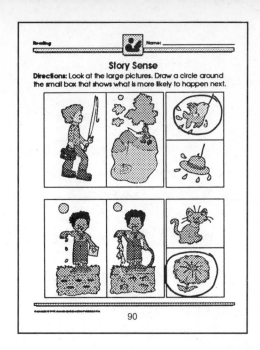

Story Sense

Directions: Look at the large pictures. Draw a circle around the small box that shows what is more likely to happen next.

90

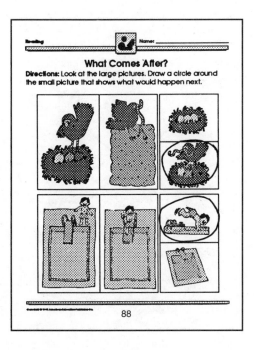

What Comes After?

Directions: Look at the large pictures. Draw a circle around the small picture that shows what would happen next.

88

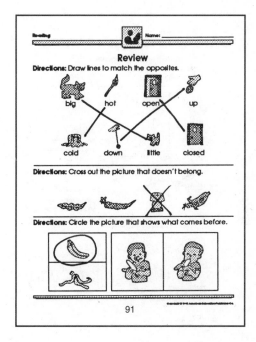

Review

Directions: Draw lines to match the opposites.

big   hot   open   up

cold   down   little   closed

Directions: Cross out the picture that doesn't belong.

Directions: Circle the picture that shows what comes before.

91

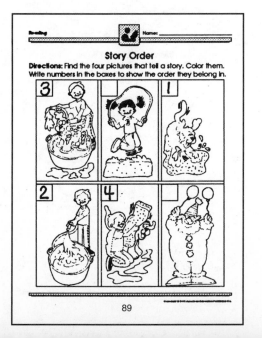

Story Order

Directions: Find the four pictures that tell a story. Color them. Write numbers in the boxes to show the order they belong in.

89

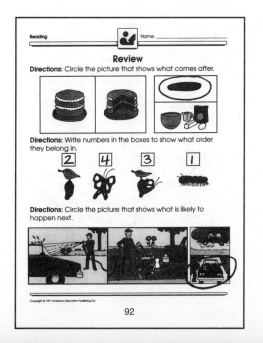

Review

Directions: Circle the picture that shows what comes after.

Directions: Write numbers in the boxes to show what order they belong in.

2   4   3   1

Directions: Circle the picture that shows what is likely to happen next.

92

321

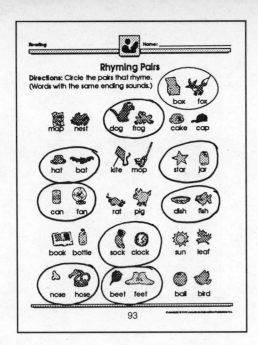

Rhyming Pairs
Directions: Circle the pairs that rhyme.
(Words with the same ending sounds.)

box fox
map nest
dog frog
cake cap
hat bat
kite mop
star jar
can fan
rat pig
dish fish
book bottle
sock clock
sun leaf
nose hose
beet feet
ball bird

93

Words That Start With L
Directions: Color the picture in each box that starts like lamb.

96

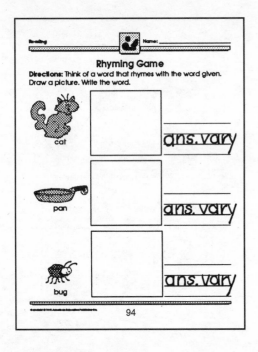

Rhyming Game
Directions: Think of a word that rhymes with the word given.
Draw a picture. Write the word.

cat — ans. vary

pan — ans. vary

bug — ans. vary

94

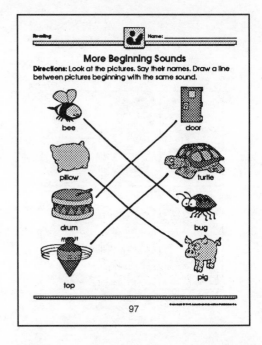

More Beginning Sounds
Directions: Look at the pictures. Say their names. Draw a line
between pictures beginning with the same sound.

bee   door
pillow   turtle
drum   bug
top   pig

97

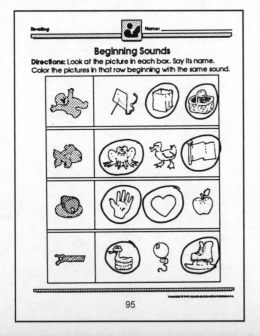

Beginning Sounds
Directions: Look at the picture in each box. Say its name.
Color the pictures in that row beginning with the same sound.

95

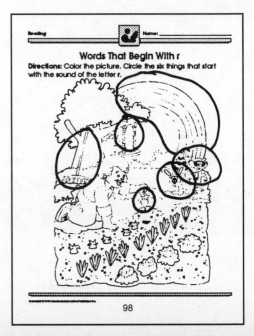

Words That Begin With r
Directions: Color the picture. Circle the six things that start
with the sound of the letter r.

98

322

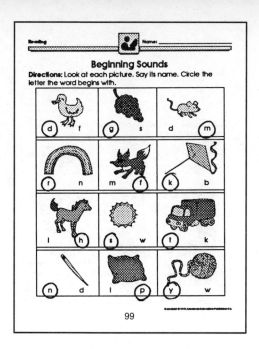

Beginning Sounds
Directions: Look at each picture. Say its name. Circle the letter the word begins with.

99

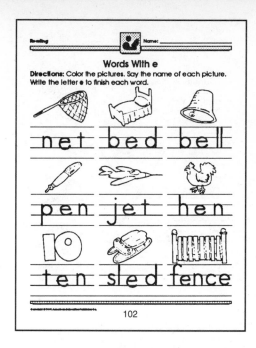

Words With e
Directions: Color the pictures. Say the name of each picture. Write the letter e to finish each word.

net   bed   bell
pen   jet   hen
ten   sled   fence

102

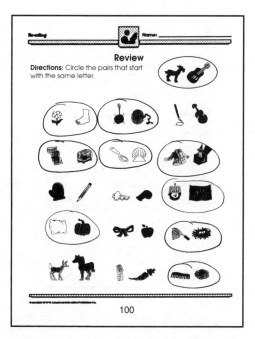

Review
Directions: Circle the pairs that start with the same letter.

100

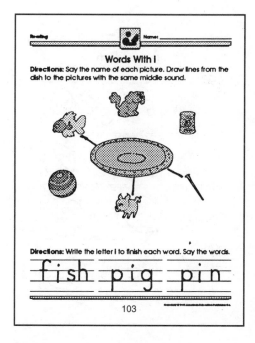

Words With i
Directions: Say the name of each picture. Draw lines from the dish to the pictures with the same middle sound.

Directions: Write the letter i to finish each word. Say the words.

fish   pig   pin

103

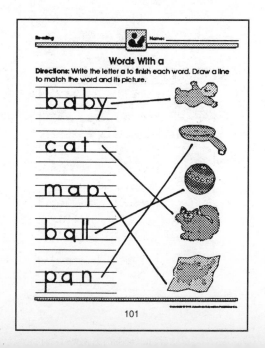

Words With a
Directions: Write the letter a to finish each word. Draw a line to match the word and its picture.

baby
cat
map
ball
pan

101

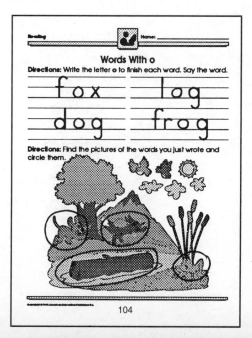

Words With o
Directions: Write the letter o to finish each word. Say the word.

fox   log
dog   frog

Directions: Find the pictures of the words you just wrote and circle them.

104

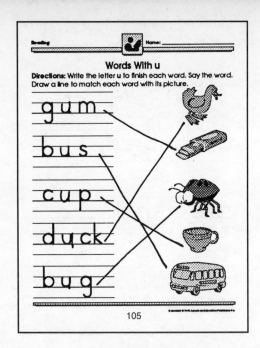

Words With u

Directions: Write the letter u to finish each word. Say the word. Draw a line to match each word with its picture.

gum
bus
cup
duck
bug

105

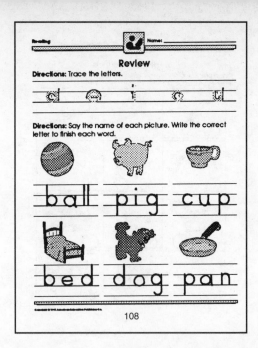

Review

Directions: Trace the letters.

Directions: Say the name of each picture. Write the correct letter to finish each word.

ball   pig   cup

bed   dog   pan

108

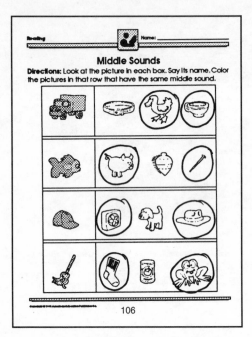

Middle Sounds

Directions: Look at the picture in each box. Say its name. Color the pictures in that row that have the same middle sound.

106

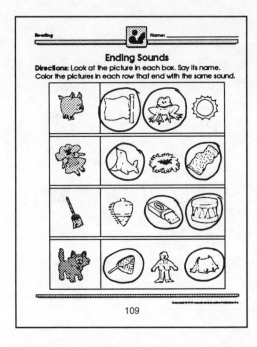

Ending Sounds

Directions: Look at the picture in each box. Say its name. Color the pictures in each row that end with the same sound.

109

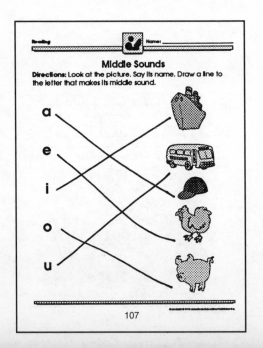

Middle Sounds

Directions: Look at the picture. Say its name. Draw a line to the letter that makes its middle sound.

a
e
i
o
u

107

324

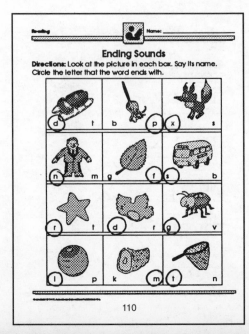

Ending Sounds

Directions: Look at the picture in each box. Say its name. Circle the letter that the word ends with.

110

Word Families

Directions: Say the name of the picture in the box. Color the pictures in each row that have the same ending sound.

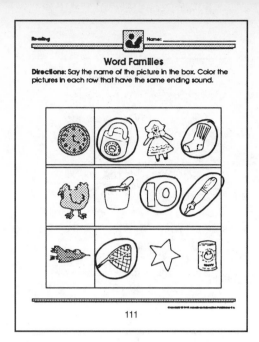

111

Words That End With an

Directions: Say the name of each picture. Draw a line to match each picture with its word.

fan

can

pan

Directions: Can you write the word that matches this picture?

man

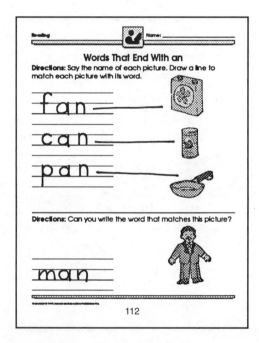

112

Words That End With at

Directions: Say the name of the picture. Trace the word.

hat

Directions: Write these words that end the same as hat.

rat

bat

Directions: Can you think of another word that sounds like hat? Write the word. Draw the picture.

ans. vary

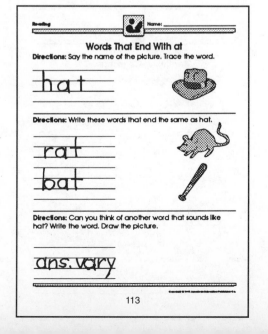

113

Review

Directions: Trace the words.

fat   red   big

Directions: Look at each picture. Say the word. Pick a word from the top with the same ending as the word in the picture. Write the words to finish the sentences.

The bed is red.

The pig is big.

The cat is fat.

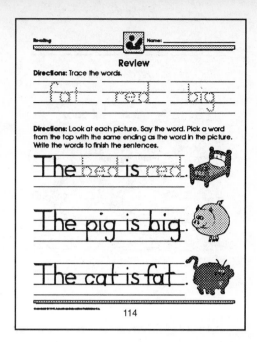

114

Beginning Consonant Ff

Find the number on the firefighter's truck.

F f   firefighter

Directions: Say each picture name. If the picture name begins with the same sound as **firefighter**, color the space.

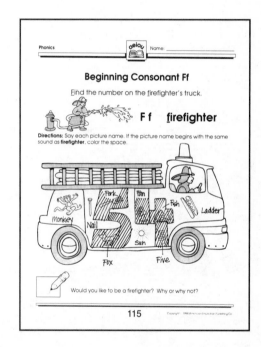

Would you like to be a firefighter? Why or why not?

115

Beginning Consonant Mm

How many monkeys meet at the movie?

M m   monkeys

Directions: Cut out the pictures at the bottom. Paste them beside things in the picture whose names begin with the same sound as **monkeys**.

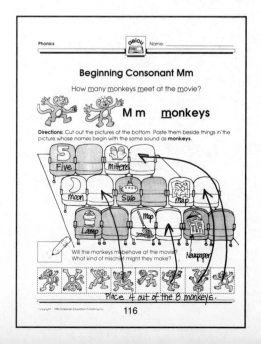

Will the monkeys misbehave at the movie? What kind of mischief might they make?

Place 4 out of the 8 monkeys.

116

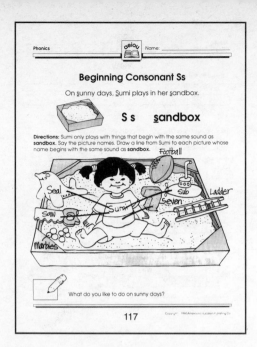

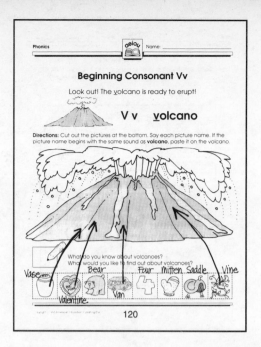

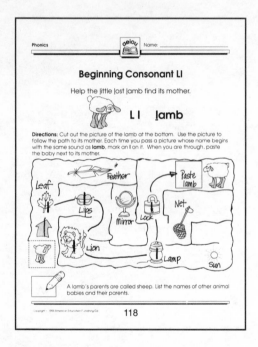

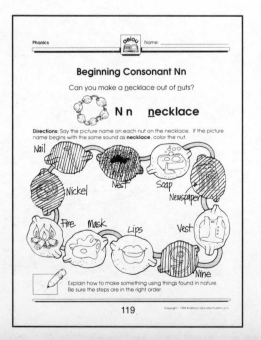

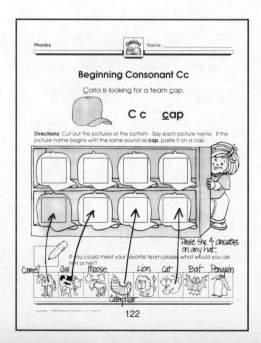

Beginning Consonant Pp

Come to Pete's pizza party!

P p   pizza

Directions: Pete is so picky he only serves foods whose names begin with the same sound as **pizza** at his party. What else does Pete serve? Say the picture names. Draw a line from Pete to each picture whose name begins with the same sound as **pizza**.

What foods would you serve at a party? Plan a menu. Ask if you can use the menu for your next birthday party?

123

Reviewing Beginning Consonants

Directions: Say each picture name. Circle the letter that stands for the beginning sound.

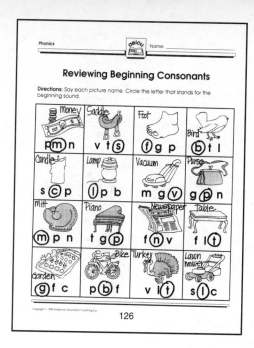

126

Beginning Consonant Tt

Tune in to your favorite television show.

T t   television

Directions: Cut out the pictures at the bottom. Say each picture name. If the picture name begins with the same sound as **television**, paste it on the television.

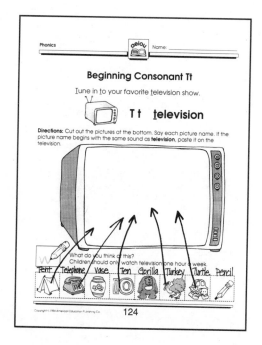

What do you think of this? Children should only watch television one hour a week.

Tent   Telephone   Vase   Ten   Gorilla   Turkey   Turtle   Pencil

124

Short Vowel a

How many people can fit in a van?

van

Directions: Short **a** is the sound you hear in the middle of the word **van**. Pretend your finger is a van at the top of the hill. Smoothly move your finger down the hill as you blend the letter sounds to read each word. Then write the word on the line.

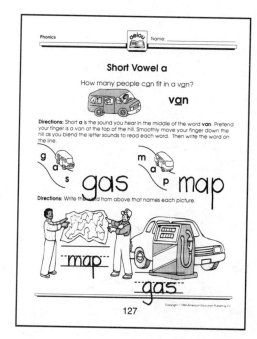

g a   s   **gas**   m a   P   **map**

Directions: Write the word from above that names each picture.

map

gas

127

Beginning Consonant Gg

What gift did the girl get?

G g   gift

Directions: Say each picture name. Color the space if the picture name begins with the same sound as **gift**.

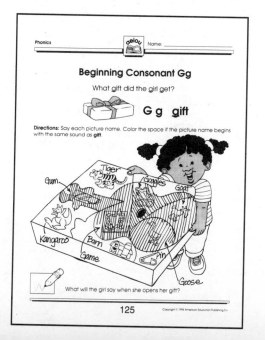

Gum   Tiger   Goggles   Goat   Kangaroo   Barn   Game   Goose

What will the girl say when she opens her gift?

125

Short Vowel i

This pig likes to dig and dig.

pig

Directions: Short **i** is the sound you hear in the middle of the word **pig**. Say each picture name. Write **i** if you hear the short **i** sound.

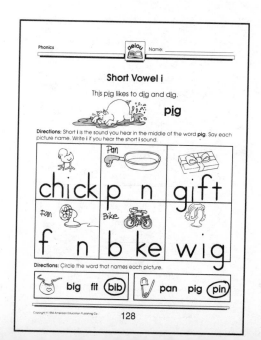

chick   p _ n   gift

f _ n   b _ ke   wig

Directions: Circle the word that names each picture.

big   fit   **bib**   pan   pig   **pin**

128

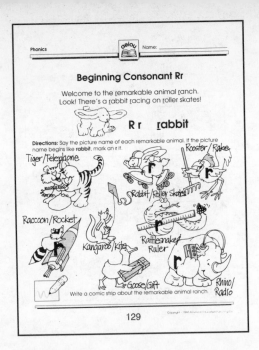

Beginning Consonant Rr

Welcome to the remarkable animal ranch.
Look! There's a rabbit racing on roller skates!

R r   rabbit

Directions: Say the picture name of each remarkable animal. If the picture name begins like **rabbit**, mark an r it.

Tiger/Telephone
Rooster/Rake
Rabbit/Roller skates
Raccoon/Rocket
Kangaroo/Kite
Rattlesnake/Ruler
Goose/Gift
Rhino/Radio

Write a comic strip about the remarkable animal ranch.

129

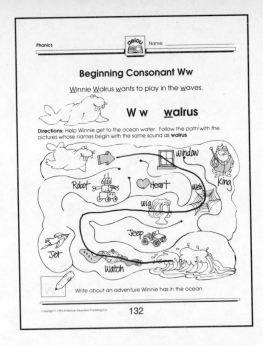

Beginning Consonant Ww

Winnie Walrus wants to play in the waves.

W w   walrus

Directions: Help Winnie get to the ocean water. Follow the path with the pictures whose names begin with the same sound as **walrus**.

window
Robot
Heart
Web
King
wig
Jeep
Jet
Watch

Write about an adventure Winnie has in the ocean.

132

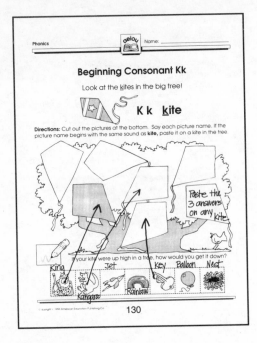

Beginning Consonant Kk

Look at the kites in the big tree!

K k   kite

Directions: Cut out the pictures at the bottom. Say each picture name. If the picture name begins with the same sound as **kite**, paste it on a kite in the tree.

Paste the 3 answers on any kite

If your kite were up high in a tree, how would you get it down?

King
Jet
Key
Balloon
Nest
Kangaroo
Rainbow

130

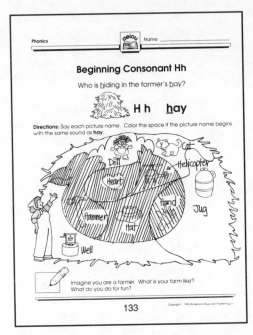

Beginning Consonant Hh

Who is hiding in the farmer's hay?

H h   hay

Directions: Say each picture name. Color the space if the picture name begins with the same sound as **hay**.

Cat
Doll
Helicopter
Heart
Hand
Hammer
Jug
Hat
Well

Imagine you are a farmer. What is your farm like? What do you do for fun?

133

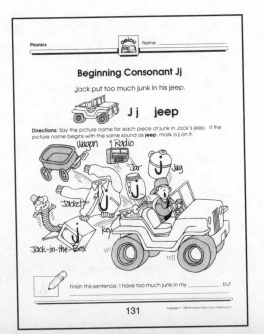

Beginning Consonant Jj

Jack put too much junk in his jeep.

J j   jeep

Directions: Say the picture name for each piece of junk in Jack's jeep. If the picture name begins with the same sound as **jeep**, mark a j on it.

Wagon
Radio
Jar
Jug
Jacket
Key
Jack-in-the-Box

Finish this sentence: I have too much junk in my _____ , but

131

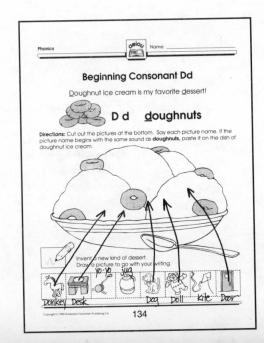

Beginning Consonant Dd

Doughnut ice cream is my favorite dessert!

D d   doughnuts

Directions: Cut out the pictures at the bottom. Say each picture name. If the picture name begins with the same sound as **doughnuts**, paste it on the dish of doughnut ice cream.

Invent a new kind of dessert. Draw a picture to go with your writing.

Donkey
Desk
yo-yo
Jug
Dog
Doll
Kite
Door

134

328

Beginning Consonant Yy

Yuriko knits a yarn blanket for her great grandson.

Y y   yarn

Directions: Say the picture names in each square on Yuriko's blanket. Circle the picture whose name begins with the same sound as **yarn**.

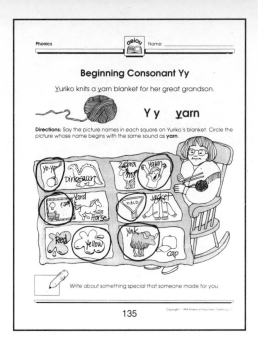

Write about something special that someone made for you.

135

Ending Consonant x

Re**x** is si**x** today.

X x   six

Directions: The word **six ends** with the sounds that the letter **x** stands for. Help Rex get to his birthday cake. Follow the path with the pictures whose names **end** with the same sounds as **six**.

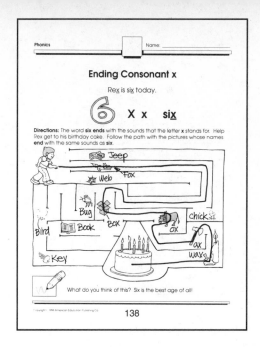

What do you think of this? Six is the best age of all!

138

Beginning Sounds Qu/qu

How quickly can you decorate the queen's crown?

Qu qu   queen

Directions: Cut out the pictures at the bottom. Say each picture name. If the picture name begins with the same sounds as **queen**, paste it on her crown.

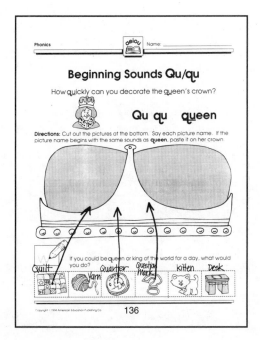

If you could be queen or king of the world for a day, what would you do?

Quilt   Yarn   Quarter   Question Mark   Kitten   Desk

136

Reviewing Beginning Consonants

Directions: Look at the letters in the boxes. Then say each picture name. Draw a line from the letter to the picture whose name begins with the sound that the letter stands for.

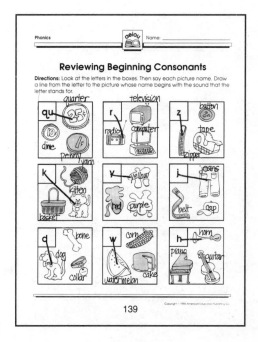

139

Beginning Consonant Zz

Step inside the zany zoo!

Z z   zoo

Directions: Circle three zany pictures whose names begin with the same sound as **zoo**.

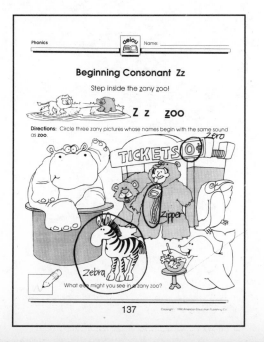

What else might you see in a zany zoo?

137

Ending Consonants

Directions: Say each picture name. Fill in the circle next to the letter that stands for the last sound.

Example:
- ○ p
- ○ d
- ○ m

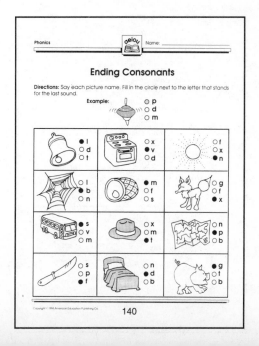

140

329

Consonant Blends

The frog stopped on the plant.

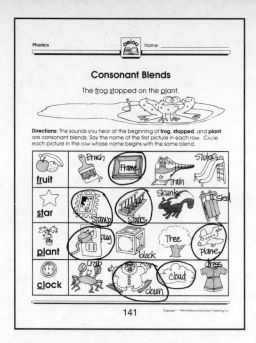

Directions: The sounds you hear at the beginning of **frog**, **stopped**, and **plant** are consonant blends. Say the name of the first picture in each row. Circle each picture in the row whose name begins with the same blend.

141

Short Vowel e

The little spider left its web.

web

Directions: Short **e** is the sound you hear in the middle of the word **web**. Circle the word that will complete each sentence. Read the sentence again to be sure that it makes sense. Then write the word on the line.

1. Peg will get in   bed .   (bed) web hen
2. Ed fed his   pet .   peg pot (pet)
3. A red hen is in a   pen .   (pen) peg pep
4. Bev has a wet   leg .   let (leg) led
5. The ten men get on the   jet . (jet) met bet
6. Chet sat on the top   step .   pep stop (step)
7. Get the bug in the   net .   not (net) nut

144

Short Vowel o

The fox hops over the log.

log

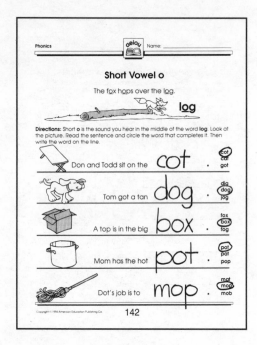

Directions: Short **o** is the sound you hear in the middle of the word **log**. Look at the picture. Read the sentence and circle the word that completes it. Then write the word on the line.

Don and Todd sit on the   cot .   (cot) cat got
Tom got a tan   dog .   dig (dog) log
A top is in the big   box .   fox (box) fog
Mom has the hot   pot .   (pot) pat pop
Dot's job is to   mop .   mat (mop) mob

142

Sound Pattern -an

Can you make a fan?

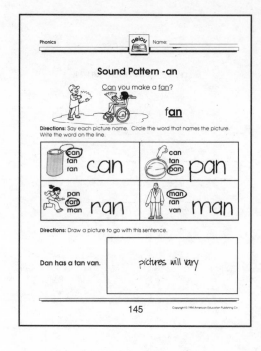

fan

Directions: Say each picture name. Circle the word that names the picture. Write the word on the line.

(can) tan ran **can**	can tan (pan) **pan**
pan (ran) man **ran**	(man) ran van **man**

Directions: Draw a picture to go with this sentence.

Dan has a tan van.   pictures will vary

145

Short Vowel u

Would you like to hug the pup?

pup

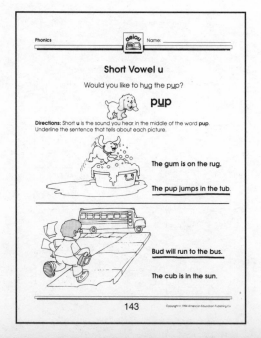

Directions: Short **u** is the sound you hear in the middle of the word **pup**. Underline the sentence that tells about each picture.

The gum is on the rug.

The pup jumps in the tub.

Bud will run to the bus.

The cub is in the sun.

143

Sound Pattern -it

Kit will sit and read a little flip book.

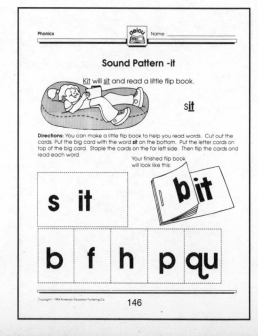

sit

Directions: You can make a little flip book to help you read words. Cut out the cards. Put the big card with the word **sit** on the bottom. Put the letter cards on top of the big card. Staple the cards on the far left side. Then flip the cards and read each word.

Your finished flip book will look like this:

s   it   b it

b   f   h   p   qu

146

330

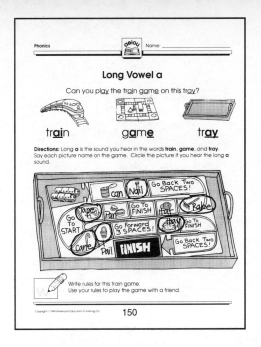

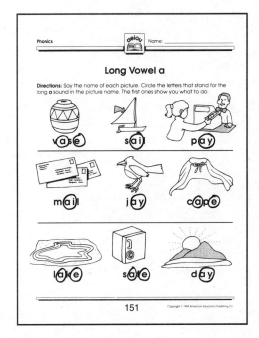

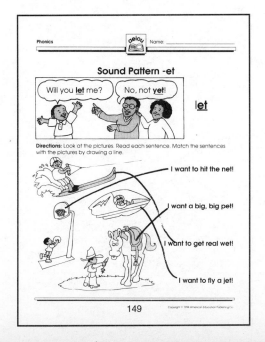

Long Vowel i

Directions: Words that have the same ending sounds are called rhyming words. Read the words on each kite. Color the kites that have three rhyming long i words.

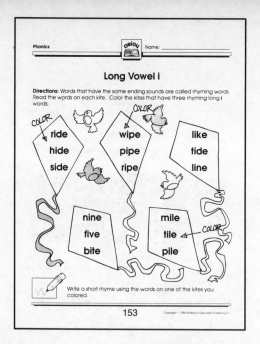

COLOR

ride
hide
side

COLOR

wipe
pipe
ripe

like
tide
line

nine
five
bite

mile
tile
pile
COLOR

Write a short rhyme using the words on one of the kites you colored.

153

Long Vowel u

The cute cub sits on a cube.

cube

Directions: Long **u** is the sound you hear in the word **cube**. Cut out the pictures at the bottom. Say each picture name. Paste the pictures whose names have the long **u** sound on the cube.

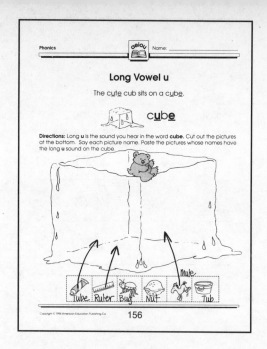

Mule

Tube   Ruler   Bug   Nut   Tub

156

Long Vowel o

Joan loads a rope on her boat.

rope   boat

Directions: Long **o** is the sound you hear in the words **rope** and **boat**. Joan only loads things on her boat whose names have the long **o** sound. Say the picture names. Draw a line from the boat to each picture whose name has the long **o** sound.

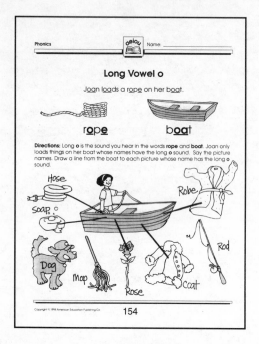

Hose

Robe

Soap

Rod

Dog

Mop

Rose

Coat

154

Long Vowel u

Directions: Look at the pictures. Read the words. Draw a line from each word to the picture it tells about.

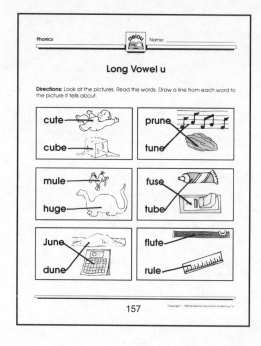

cute
cube

prune
tune

mule
huge

fuse
tube

June
dune

flute
rule

157

Long Vowel o

Directions: Say the name of each picture. Finish the name by writing o and e or oa when you hear the long o sound.

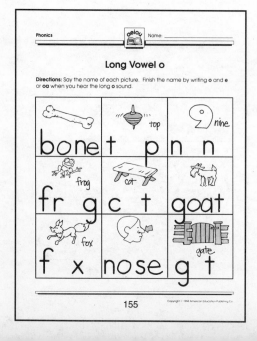

bone t	top — p n n	nine —
frog — fr g	cot — c t	goat
fox — f x	nose	gate — g t

155

Long Vowel e

What does the team see in the tree?

team   tree

Directions: Long **e** is the sound you hear in the words **team** and **tree**. Say each picture name on the tree. Color the space if the picture name has the long **e** sound.

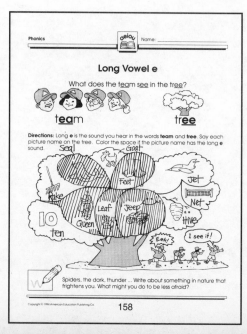

Seal   Goat   Feet   Jet

Rake   Net

10   Leaf   Jeep   Hive

ten   Queen

Eek!   I see it!

Spiders, the dark, thunder ... Write about something in nature that frightens you. What might you do to be less afraid?

158

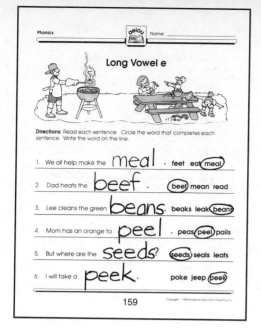

Long Vowel e

Directions: Read each sentence. Circle the word that completes each sentence. Write the word on the line.

1. We all help make the **meal** . feet eat (meal)

2. Dad heats the **beef** . (beef) mean read

3. Lee cleans the green **beans** . beaks leak (beans)

4. Mom has an orange to **peel** . peas (peel) pails

5. But where are the **seeds**? (seeds) seals leafs

6. I will take a **peek** . poke jeep (peek)

159

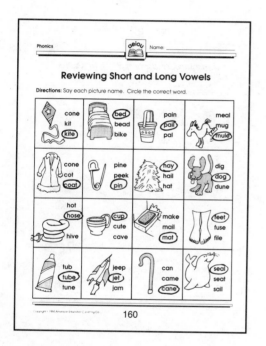

Reviewing Short and Long Vowels

Directions: Say each picture name. Circle the correct word.

cone / kit / (kite)	(bed) / bead / bike	pain / (pail) / pal	meal / mug / (mule)
cone / cot / (coat)	pine / peek / (pin)	(hay) / hail / hat	dig / (dog) / dune
hot / (hose) / hive	(cup) / cute / (mat)	make / mail	(feet) / fuse / file
tub / (tube) / tune	jeep / (jet) / jam	can / came / (cane)	(seal) / seat / sail

160

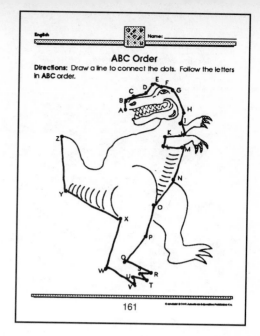

ABC Order

Directions: Draw a line to connect the dots. Follow the letters in ABC order.

161

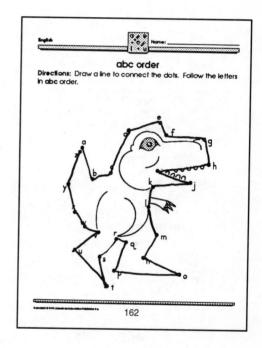

abc order

Directions: Draw a line to connect the dots. Follow the letters in abc order.

162

333

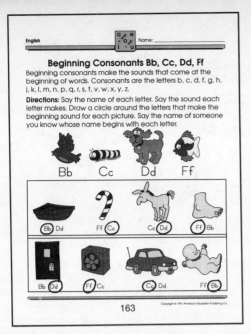

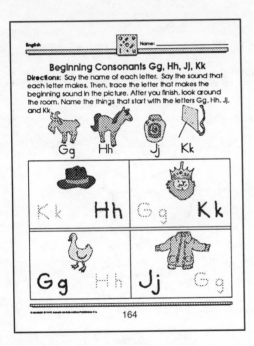

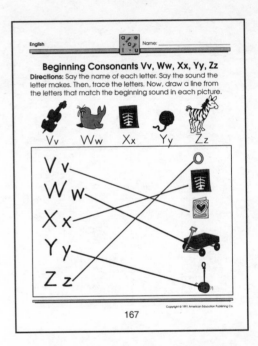

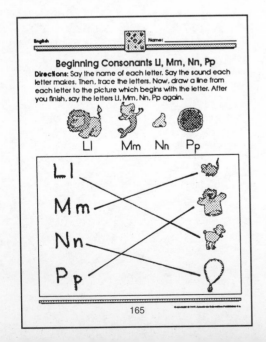

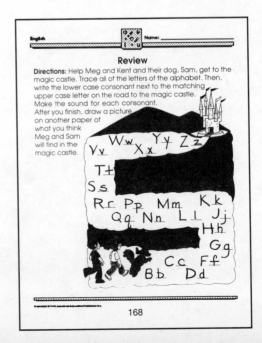

334

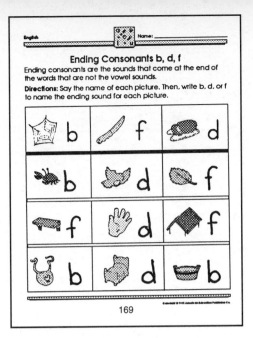

Ending Consonants b, d, f

Ending consonants are the sounds that come at the end of the words that are not the vowel sounds.

Directions: Say the name of each picture. Then, write b, d, or f to name the ending sound for each picture.

169

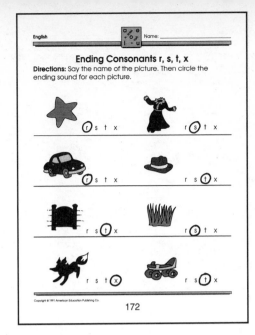

Ending Consonants r, s, t, x

Directions: Say the name of the picture. Then circle the ending sound for each picture.

172

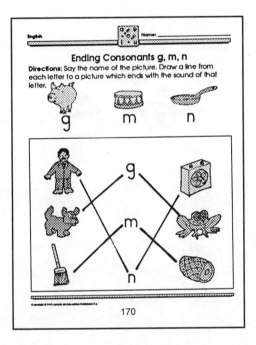

Ending Consonants g, m, n

Directions: Say the name of the picture. Draw a line from each letter to a picture which ends with the sound of that letter.

170

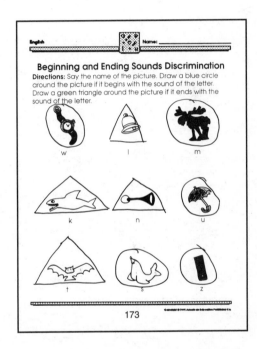

Beginning and Ending Sounds Discrimination

Directions: Say the name of the picture. Draw a blue circle around the picture if it begins with the sound of the letter. Draw a green triangle around the picture if it ends with the sound of the letter.

173

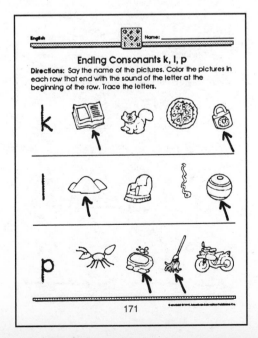

Ending Consonants k, l, p

Directions: Say the name of the pictures. Color the pictures in each row that end with the sound of the letter at the beginning of the row. Trace the letters.

171

Beginning and Ending Sounds Discrimination

Directions: Say the name of each picture. Draw a triangle around the letter that makes the beginning sound. Draw a square around the letter that makes the ending sound. Color the pictures.

174

Beginning and Ending Sounds Discrimination

Directions: Look at the example. Say the beginning and ending sounds for the word pipe. Write the letter that makes the beginning and ending sound for each picture.

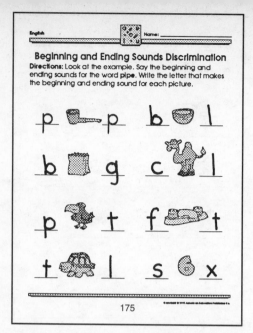

Review

Directions: Say the name of each object which has a consonant near it. Color the object orange if it begins with the sound of the letter. Color the object purple if it ends with the sound of the letter.

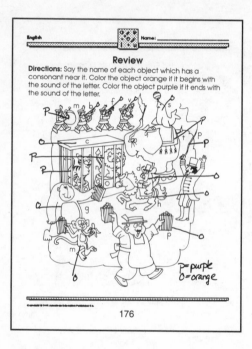

p = purple
O = orange

Short Vowel Sounds

The short vowel sounds used in this book are found in the following words: ant, egg, igloo, on, up.

Directions: Say the name of each picture. The short vowel sound may be in the front of the word or in the middle of the word. Color the pictures in each row that have the correct short vowel sound.

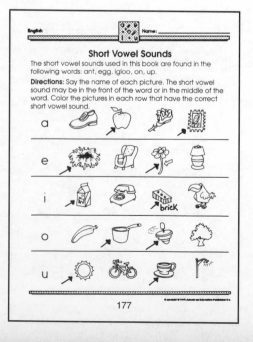

Long Vowel Sounds

Long vowel sounds say their own name. The following words have long vowel sounds: hay, me, pie, no, cute.

Directions: Say the name of each picture. Color the pictures in each row that have the correct long vowel sound.

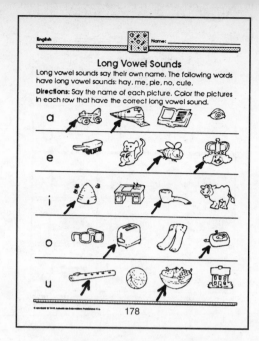

Discrimination Of Short And Long Aa

Directions: Say the name of each picture. If it has the short $\breve{a}$ sound, color it red. If it has the long $\bar{a}$ sound, color it yellow.

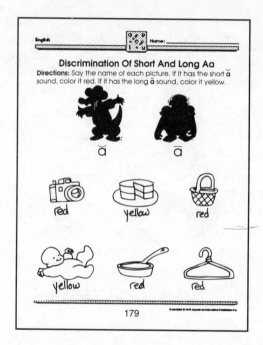

Discrimination Of Short And Long Ee

Directions: Say the name of each picture. Draw a circle around the pictures which have the short $\breve{e}$ sound. Draw a triangle around the pictures which have the long $\bar{e}$ sound.

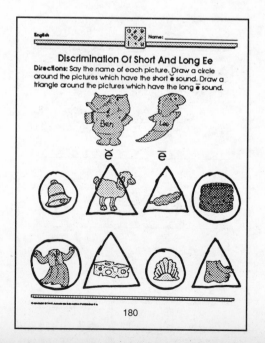

Discrimination Of Short And Long Ii.

Directions: Say the name of each picture. Color it yellow if it has the short **i** sound. Color it red if it has the long **i** sound.

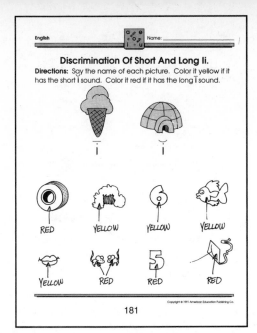

181

Short And Long Vowel Sounds

Directions: Say the name of the picture. Write the correct vowel on each line to finish the word. Color the short vowel pictures yellow. Circle the long vowel pictures.

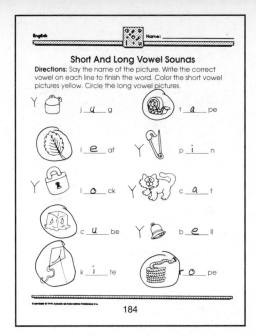

184

Discrimination Of Short And Long Oo

Directions: Say the name of each picture. If the picture has a long **o** sound, write a green **L** in the space. If the picture has a short **o** sound, write a red **S** in the space.

182

ABC Order

Use the first letter of each word to put the words in alphabetical order.

Directions: Draw a circle around the first letter of each word. Then, put the words in ABC order.

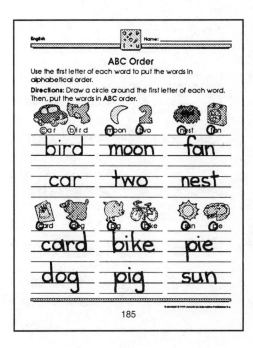

185

Discrimination Of Short And Long Uu

Directions: Say the name of the picture. If it has the long **u** sound, write a u in the unicorn column. If it has a short **u** sound, write a u in the umbrella column.

183

337

ABC Order

Directions: Circle the first letter of each animal's name. Write a 1, 2, 3, 4, 5, or 6 on the line next to the animals' names to put the words in ABC order.

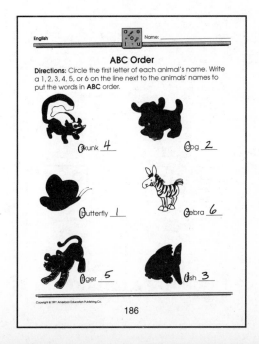

186

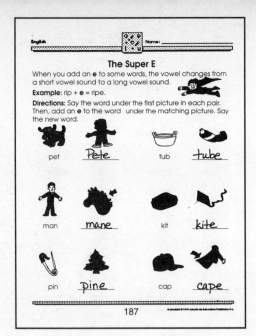

The Super E

When you add an **e** to some words, the vowel changes from a short vowel sound to a long vowel sound.

Example: rip + e = ripe.

Directions: Say the word under the first picture in each pair. Then, add an **e** to the word under the matching picture. Say the new word.

pet — *Pete*   tub — *tube*

man — *mane*   kit — *kite*

pin — *pine*   cap — *cape*

187

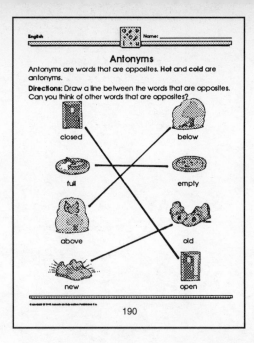

Antonyms

Antonyms are words that are opposites. **Hot** and **cold** are antonyms.

Directions: Draw a line between the words that are opposites. Can you think of other words that are opposites?

closed — below
full — empty
above — old
new — open

190

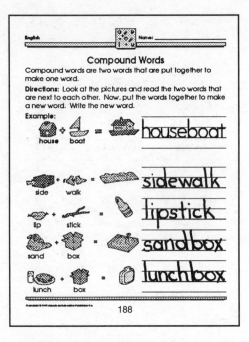

Compound Words

Compound words are two words that are put together to make one word.

Directions: Look at the pictures and read the two words that are next to each other. Now, put the words together to make a new word. Write the new word.

Example:

house + boat = *houseboat*

side + walk = *sidewalk*

lip + stick = *lipstick*

sand + box = *sandbox*

lunch + box = *lunchbox*

188

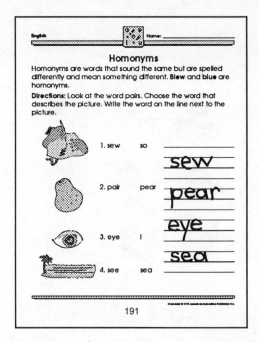

Homonyms

Homonyms are words that sound the same but are spelled differently and mean something different. **Blew** and **blue** are homonyms.

Directions: Look at the word pairs. Choose the word that describes the picture. Write the word on the line next to the picture.

1. sew   so   *sew*
2. pair   pear   *pear*
3. eye   I   *eye*
4. see   sea   *sea*

191

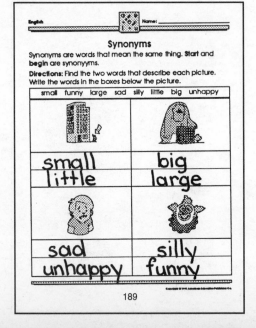

Synonyms

Synonyms are words that mean the same thing. **Start** and **begin** are synonyms.

Directions: Find the two words that describe each picture. Write the words in the boxes below the picture.

small funny large sad silly little big unhappy

small / *little*   *big* / *large*

sad / *unhappy*   *silly* / *funny*

189

338

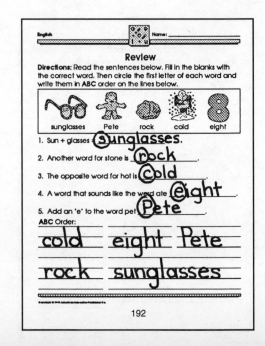

Review

Directions: Read the sentences below. Fill in the blanks with the correct word. Then circle the first letter of each word and write them in ABC order on the lines below.

sunglasses   Pete   rock   cold   eight

1. Sun + glasses = *sunglasses*.
2. Another word for stone is *rock*.
3. The opposite word for hot is *cold*.
4. A word that sounds like the word ate is *eight*.
5. Add an 'e' to the word pet *Pete*

ABC Order:

cold   *eight*   *Pete*

rock   *sunglasses*

192

Nouns Are Naming Words

Nouns tell the name of a person, place, or thing.

Directions: Look at each picture. Color it red if it names a person. Color it blue if it names a place. Color it green if it names a thing.

193

More Than One

Directions: Read the nouns under the pictures. Then, write the noun under One or More Than One.

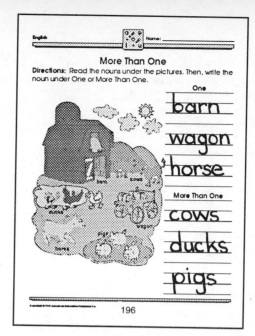

One

barn

wagon

horse

More Than One

cows

ducks

pigs

196

Nouns Are Naming Words

Directions: Write these naming words in the correct box.

| store | zoo | child | baby | teacher | table |
| cat | park | gym | woman | sock | horse |

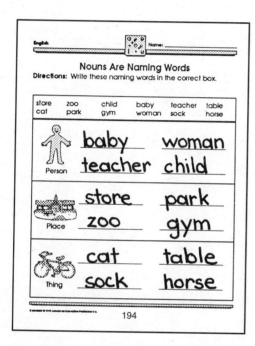

Person	baby woman
	teacher child
Place	store park
	zoo gym
Thing	cat table
	sock horse

194

Verbs Are Action Words

Verbs are words that tell what a person or a thing can do.

Example: The girl pats the dog.
The word "pat" is the verb. It shows action.

Directions: Draw a line between the verbs and the pictures that show the action.

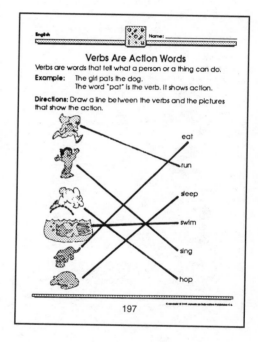

eat

run

sleep

swim

sing

hop

197

More Than One

Some nouns name more than one person, place or thing.

Directions: Add an "s" to make the words tell about the picture.

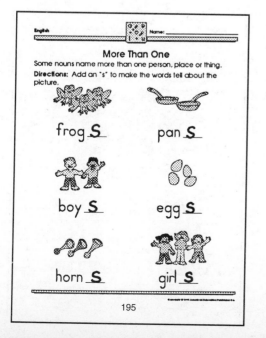

frog **S**   pan **S**

boy **S**   egg **S**

horn **S**   girl **S**

195

Verbs Are Action Words.

Directions:
Look at the pictures. Read the words. Write an action word in each sentence below.

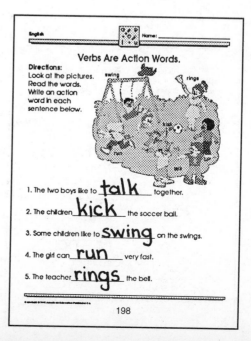

1. The two boys like to **talk** together.

2. The children **kick** the soccer ball.

3. Some children like to **swing** on the swings.

4. The girl can **run** very fast.

5. The teacher **rings** the bell.

198

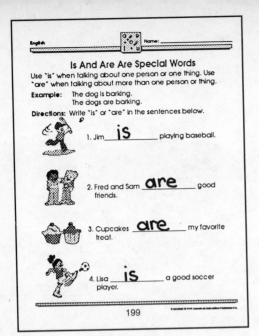

Is And Are Are Special Words

Use "is" when talking about one person or one thing. Use "are" when talking about more than one person or thing.

Example: The dog is barking.
The dogs are barking.

Directions: Write "is" or "are" in the sentences below.

1. Jim **is** playing baseball.

2. Fred and Sam **are** good friends.

3. Cupcakes **are** my favorite treat.

4. Lisa **is** a good soccer player.

199

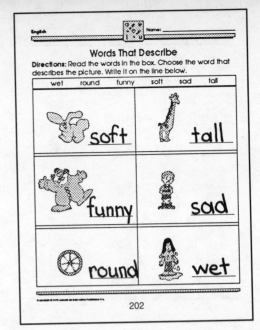

Words That Describe

Directions: Read the words in the box. Choose the word that describes the picture. Write it on the line below.

wet	round	funny	soft	sad	tall

soft — tall

funny — sad

round — wet

202

Nouns And Verbs

Directions: Read the sentences below. Draw a red circle around the nouns. Draw a blue line under the verbs.

1. The boy runs fast.

2. The turtle eats leaves.

3. The fish swim in the tank.

4. The girl hits the ball.

200

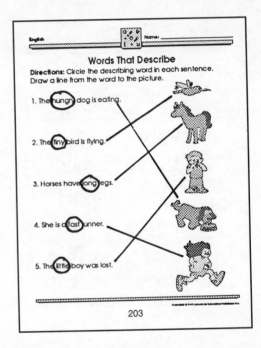

Words That Describe

Directions: Circle the describing word in each sentence. Draw a line from the word to the picture.

1. The hungry dog is eating.

2. The tiny bird is flying.

3. Horses have long legs.

4. She is a fast runner.

5. The little boy was lost.

203

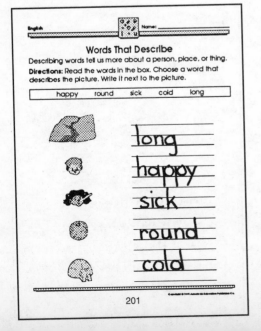

Words That Describe

Describing words tell us more about a person, place, or thing.

Directions: Read the words in the box. Choose a word that describes the picture. Write it next to the picture.

happy	round	sick	cold	long

long

happy

sick

round

cold

201

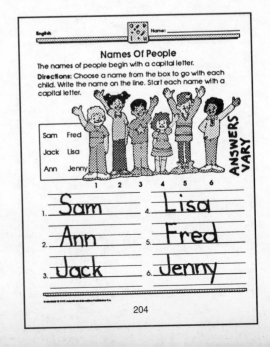

Names Of People

The names of people begin with a capital letter.

Directions: Choose a name from the box to go with each child. Write the name on the line. Start each name with a capital letter.

Sam	Fred
Jack	Lisa
Ann	Jenny

ANSWERS VARY

1. Sam   4. Lisa

2. Ann   5. Fred

3. Jack   6. Jenny

204

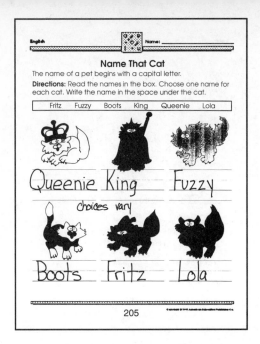

Name That Cat

The name of a pet begins with a capital letter.

Directions: Read the names in the box. Choose one name for each cat. Write the name in the space under the cat.

Fritz	Fuzzy	Boots	King	Queenie	Lola

Queenie　King　Fuzzy

choices vary

Boots　Fritz　Lola

205

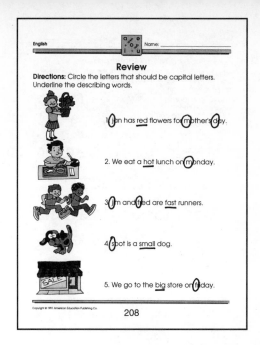

Review

Directions: Circle the letters that should be capital letters. Underline the describing words.

1. jan has red flowers for mother's day.

2. We eat a hot lunch on monday.

3. jim and fred are fast runners.

4. spot is a small dog.

5. We go to the big store on friday.

Copyright © 1991 American Education Publishing Co.

208

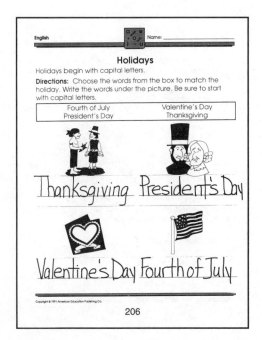

Holidays

Holidays begin with capital letters.

Directions: Choose the words from the box to match the holiday. Write the words under the picture. Be sure to start with capital letters.

Fourth of July	Valentine's Day
President's Day	Thanksgiving

Thanksgiving　President's Day

Valentine's Day　Fourth of July

Copyright © 1991 American Education Publishing Co.

206

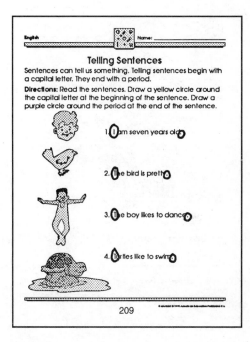

Telling Sentences

Sentences can tell us something. Telling sentences begin with a capital letter. They end with a period.

Directions: Read the sentences. Draw a yellow circle around the capital letter at the beginning of the sentence. Draw a purple circle around the period at the end of the sentence.

1. I am seven years old.

2. The bird is pretty.

3. The boy likes to dance.

4. Turtles like to swim.

209

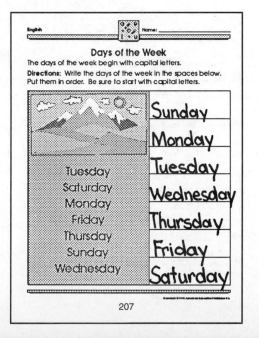

Days of the Week

The days of the week begin with capital letters.

Directions: Write the days of the week in the spaces below. Put them in order. Be sure to start with capital letters.

Tuesday
Saturday
Monday
Friday
Thursday
Sunday
Wednesday

Sunday
Monday
Tuesday
Wednesday
Thursday
Friday
Saturday

Copyright © 1991 American Education Publishing Co.

207

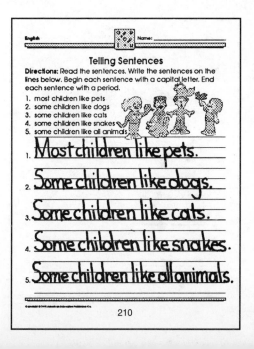

Telling Sentences

Directions: Read the sentences. Write the sentences on the lines below. Begin each sentence with a capital letter. End each sentence with a period.

1. most children like pets
2. some children like dogs
3. some children like cats
4. some children like snakes
5. some children like all animals

1. Most children like pets.

2. Some children like dogs.

3. Some children like cats.

4. Some children like snakes.

5. Some children like all animals.

Copyright © 1991 American Education Publishing Co.

210

Telling Sentences

Directions: Read the sentences. Write the sentences below. Start each sentence with a capital letter and end with a period.

1. I like to go to the store with Mom
2. we go on Friday
3. I get to push the cart
4. I get to buy the cookies
5. I like to help Mom

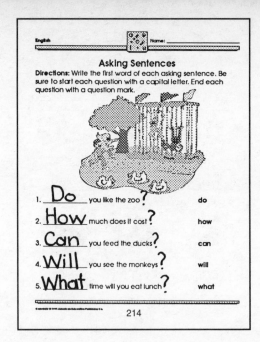

1. I like to go to the store with Mom.
2. We go on Friday.
3. I get to push the cart.
4. I get to buy the cookies.
5. I like to help Mom.

211

Asking Sentences

Directions: Write the first word of each asking sentence. Be sure to start each question with a capital letter. End each question with a question mark.

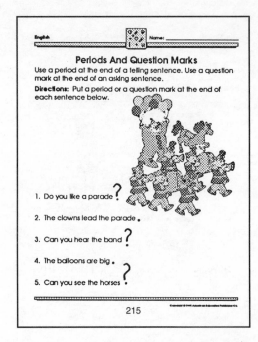

1. __Do__ you like the zoo ?   do
2. __How__ much does it cost ?   how
3. __Can__ you feed the ducks ?   can
4. __Will__ you see the monkeys ?   will
5. __What__ time will you eat lunch ?   what

214

Asking Sentences

Asking sentences ask a question. An asking sentence begins with a capital letter. It ends with a question mark.

Directions: Draw a green line under the sentences that ask a question.

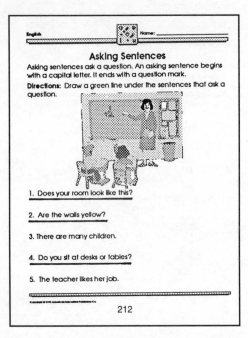

1. Does your room look like this?
2. Are the walls yellow?
3. There are many children.
4. Do you sit at desks or tables?
5. The teacher likes her job.

212

Periods And Question Marks

Use a period at the end of a telling sentence. Use a question mark at the end of an asking sentence.

Directions: Put a period or a question mark at the end of each sentence below.

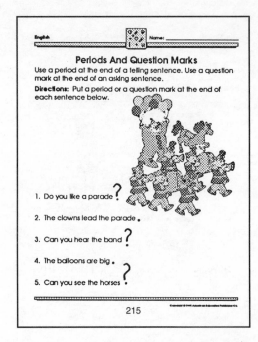

1. Do you like a parade ?
2. The clowns lead the parade .
3. Can you hear the band ?
4. The balloons are big .
5. Can you see the horses ?

215

Asking Sentences

Directions: Draw a blue line under the sentences that ask a question.

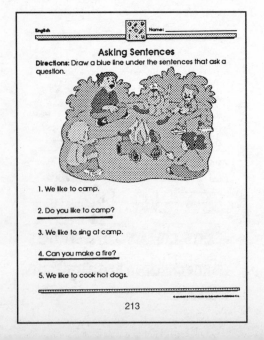

1. We like to camp.
2. Do you like to camp?
3. We like to sing at camp.
4. Can you make a fire?
5. We like to cook hot dogs.

213

Review

Directions: Look at the picture. In the space below, write one telling sentence about the picture. Then, write one asking sentence about the picture.

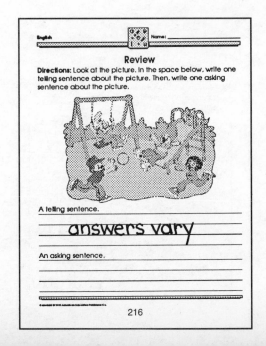

A telling sentence.

__answers vary__

An asking sentence.

216

342

Word Order

Word order is the logical order of words in a sentence.

Directions: Put the words in each sentence in order. Write the sentence on the lines.

1. We made lemonade. some
2. good. It was
3. We the sold lemonade.
4. cost it five cents.
5. fun. We had

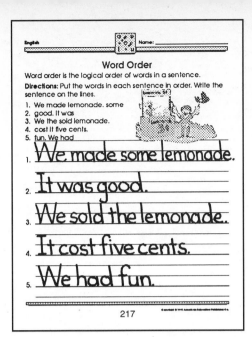

1. We made some lemonade.
2. It was good.
3. We sold the lemonade.
4. It cost five cents.
5. We had fun.

217

I Can Write Sentences

A story has more than one sentence.

Directions: Use the words from the pictures to write a story.

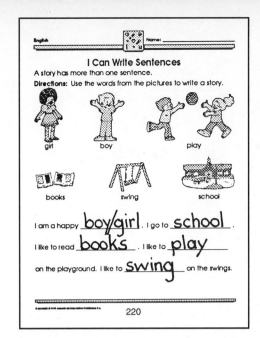

girl   boy   play

books   swing   school

I am a happy **boy/girl**. I go to **school**.
I like to read **books**. I like to **play**
on the playground. I like to **swing** on the swings.

220

Word Order

Directions: Look at the picture. Put the words in the correct order. Write the sentences on the lines below.

1. a Jan starfish. has
2. and Bill to Peg swim. like
3. The shining. sun is
4. sand. the in Jack likes play to
5. cold. water The is

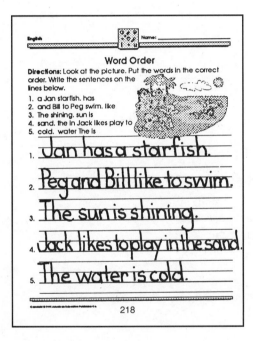

1. Jan has a starfish.
2. Peg and Bill like to swim.
3. The sun is shining.
4. Jack likes to play in the sand.
5. The water is cold.

218

I Can Write Sentences

Directions: Draw a picture of yourself in the box marked **Me**. Then write three sentences about yourself on the lines.

Me

picture varies

1. sentences vary
2. _____
3. _____

221

Word Order Can Change Meaning

If you change the order of the words in a sentence, you can change the meaning of the sentence.

Directions: Read the sentences. Draw a purple circle around the sentence that describes the picture.

Example:

The fox jumped over the dogs.
The dogs jumped over the fox.

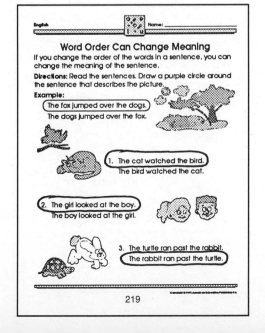

1. The cat watched the bird.
The bird watched the cat.

2. The girl looked at the boy.
The boy looked at the girl.

3. The turtle ran past the rabbit.
The rabbit ran past the turtle.

219

Review

Directions: Put the words in the right order to make a sentence. The sentences will tell a story.

1. a gerbil. has Ann
2. is The Mike. named gerbil
3. likes eat. Mike to
4. play. to Mike likes
5. happy a is gerbil. Mike

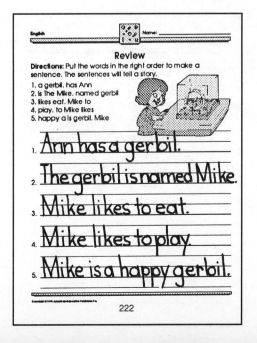

1. Ann has a gerbil.
2. The gerbil is named Mike.
3. Mike likes to eat.
4. Mike likes to play.
5. Mike is a happy gerbil.

222

343

Page 223 Words and pictures will vary.

Page 224 *Mom:* mirror, map *Dad:* pajamas, pen *Pat:* bank, book *Bill:* ball, doll

Page 225 *Possible words:* lap, lip, dig, rib, cap, fan, fin, map

Page 226 Words will vary.

Page 227 Results will vary.

Page 228 Game of checkers will vary, but students should know all the words.

Page 229 Answers will vary.

Page 230 *Words with same meanings:* little–small, silly–funny, below–under *Words with opposite meanings:* happy–sad, on–off, more–less, nice–mean, up–down; winner will vary

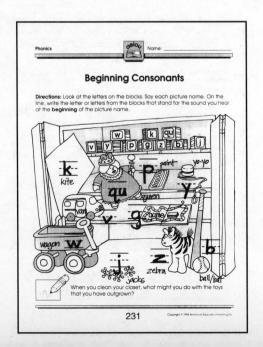

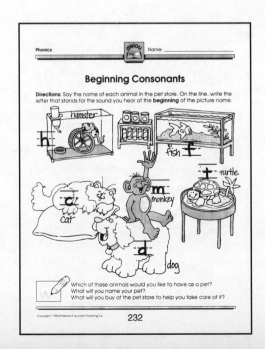

Ending Consonants

Directions: Say the name of each animal at the zoo. On the line, write the letter that stands for the sound you hear at the **end** of the picture name.

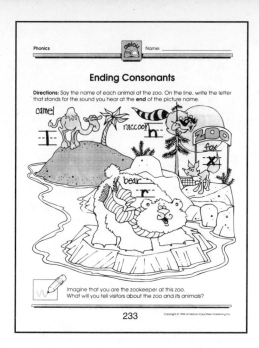

camel   l
raccoon   n
fox   x
bear   r

Imagine that you are the zookeeper at this zoo. What will you tell visitors about the zoo and its animals?

233

Short Vowels

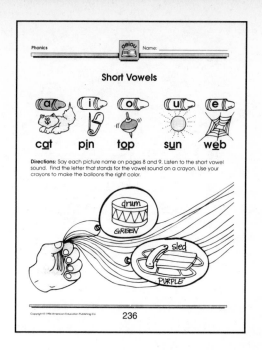

cat   pin   top   sun   web

Directions: Say each picture name on pages 8 and 9. Listen to the short vowel sound. Find the letter that stands for the vowel sound on a crayon. Use your crayons to make the balloons the right color.

drum   GREEN
sled   PURPLE

236

Middle Consonants

The letter **d** stands for the sound you hear in the middle of the word **ladder**.

Directions: Say each picture name. On the line, write the letter that stands for the sound you hear in the **middle** of the picture name.

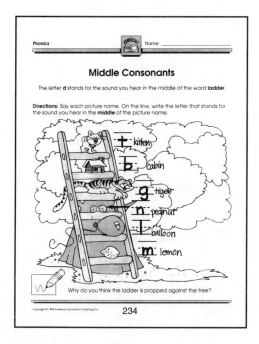

t   kitten
b   cabin
g   tiger
n   peanut
l   balloon
m   lemon

Why do you think the ladder is propped against the tree?

234

hand   RED
nest   PURPLE
ship   YELLOW
lamp   RED
brush   GREEN
mitt   YELLOW
sock   BLUE
duck   GREEN
dress   PURPLE
mask   RED
fish   YELLOW
box   BLUE

237

Beginning, Middle, and Ending Consonants

Directions: Say each picture name. In the spaces below the picture, write the letters that stand for the sounds you hear at the beginning, middle, and end of the picture name. The first one shows you what to do.

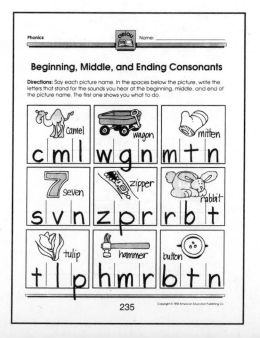

camel   c m l
wagon   w g n
mitten   m t n
seven   s v n
zipper   z p r
rabbit   r b t
tulip   t l p
hammer   h m r
button   b t n

235

Short Vowels

Directions: Say the name of each picture. Circle the picture name. Write the name. The first one shows you what to do.

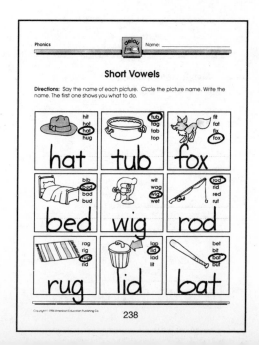

hit hot **hat** hug   **hat**
tub tag tab top   **tub**
fit fat fix **fox**   **fox**
bib **bed** bad bud   **bed**
wit wag **wig** wet   **wig**
rod rid red rut   **rod**
rag rig **rug** rid   **rug**
lap **lid** lad lit   **lid**
bet bit **bat** but   **bat**

238

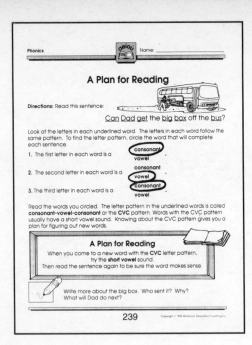

Phonics — Name: _____

A Plan for Reading

Directions: Read this sentence:

Can Dad get the big box off the bus?

Look at the letters in each underlined word. The letters in each word follow the same pattern. To find the letter pattern, circle the word that will complete each sentence.

1. The first letter in each word is a **(consonant)** / vowel

2. The second letter in each word is a consonant / **(vowel)**

3. The third letter in each word is a **(consonant)** / vowel

Read the words you circled. The letter pattern in the underlined words is called **consonant-vowel-consonant** or the **CVC** pattern. Words with the CVC pattern usually have a short vowel sound. Knowing about the CVC pattern gives you a plan for figuring out new words.

A Plan for Reading
When you come to a new word with the **CVC** letter pattern, try the **short vowel** sound. Then read the sentence again to be sure the word makes sense.

Write more about the big box. Who sent it? Why? What will Dad do next?

239

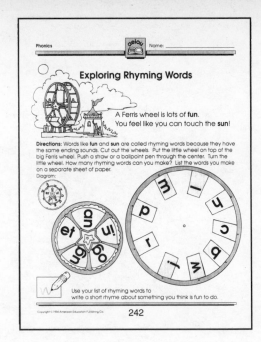

Phonics — Name: _____

Exploring Rhyming Words

A Ferris wheel is lots of **fun**.
You feel like you can touch the **sun**!

Directions: Words like **fun** and **sun** are called rhyming words because they have the same ending sounds. Cut out the wheels. Put the little wheel on top of the big Ferris wheel. Push a straw or a ballpoint pen through the center. Turn the little wheel. How many rhyming words can you make? List the words you make on a separate sheet of paper.
Diagram:

Use your list of rhyming words to write a short rhyme about something you think is fun to do.

242

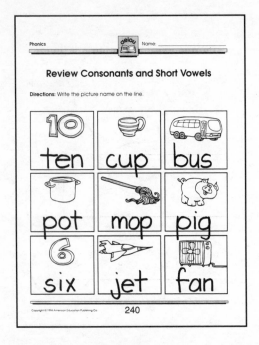

Phonics — Name: _____

Review Consonants and Short Vowels

Directions: Write the picture name on the line.

ten	cup	bus
pot	mop	pig
six	jet	fan

240

Phonics — Name: _____

Rhyming Words

Directions: Read each riddle. Write the answer on the line. Then write two words that rhyme with the answer. The first one shows you what to do.

We carry groceries in it. It holds books or our lunch, too. What is it?

bag   rag   tag

It likes to dig in the mud. It has a curly tail. What is it?

pig   big   wig

It is the number of our fingers. It is the number of our toes too! What is it?

ten   men   pen

Bunnies can do this. So can kangaroos and frogs. What is it?

hop   mop   top

Make up a riddle about one of the rhyming words. Ask a friend to solve it.

243

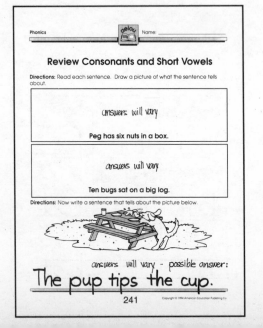

Phonics — Name: _____

Review Consonants and Short Vowels

Directions: Read each sentence. Draw a picture of what the sentence tells about.

answers will vary

Peg has six nuts in a box.

answers will vary

Ten bugs sat on a big log.

Directions: Now write a sentence that tells about the picture below.

answers will vary - possible answer:

The pup tips the cup.

241

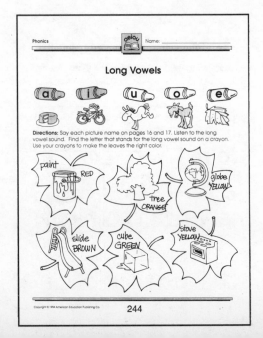

Phonics — Name: _____

Long Vowels

a   i   u   o   e

Directions: Say each picture name on pages 16 and 17. Listen to the long vowel sound. Find the letter that stands for the long vowel sound on a crayon. Use your crayons to make the leaves the right color.

paint RED
tree ORANGE
globe YELLOW
slide BROWN
cube GREEN
stove YELLOW

244

346

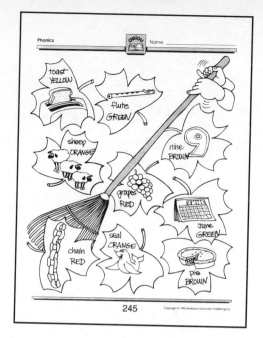

245

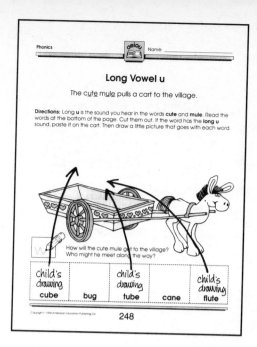

Long Vowel u

The cute mule pulls a cart to the village.

Directions: Long **u** is the sound you hear in the words **cute** and **mule**. Read the words at the bottom of the page. Cut them out. If the word has the **long u** sound, paste it on the cart. Then draw a little picture that goes with each word.

How will the cute mule get to the village? Who might he meet along the way?

| child's drawing | | child's drawing | | child's drawing |
| cube | bug | tube | cane | flute |

248

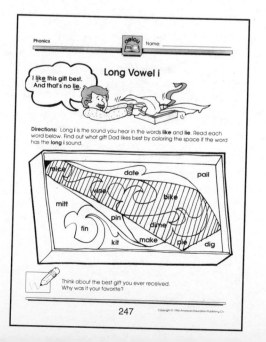

Long Vowel a

Help Jay sail across the lake to the cave.

Directions: Long **a** is the sound you hear in the words **Jay**, **sail**, and **lake**. Read the words on Jay's sail. Then look at the pictures on the maze. Use the words on the sail to label the pictures on the maze. The first one shows you what to do.

vase	mail	hay
cake	tray	rain
tape	pay	
pail		

vase · mail · hay · cake · pail · tape · rain · tray · pay

Write about an adventure Jay has when he gets to the cave.

246

Long Vowel o

Joe used a coat, a bow, and a carrot for the nose.

Directions: Long **o** is the sound you hear in the words **Joe**, **coat**, **bow**, and **nose**. Cut out the flash cards. Sort them by different spellings for the sound of **long o**. Read each word. Then make up a game to play with the cards.

| toe | soap | goat | rope |
| mow | hoe | bone | row |

249

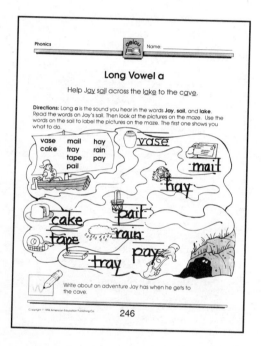

Long Vowel i

I like this gift best. And that's no lie.

Directions: Long **i** is the sound you hear in the words **like** and **lie**. Read each word below. Find out what gift Dad likes best by coloring the space if the word has the **long i** sound.

mice · date · pail · vine · bike · mitt · pin · dime · fin · kit · make · pie · dig

Think about the best gift you ever received. Why was it your favorite?

247

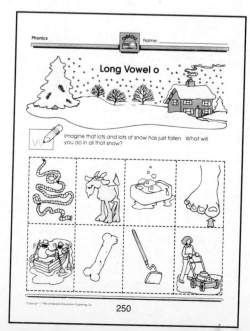

Long Vowel o

Imagine that lots and lots of snow has just fallen. What will you do in all that snow?

250

347

Long Vowel e

Take a seat in the jeep.

Directions: Long **e** is the sound you hear in the words **seat** and **jeep.** Take a ride in the jeep to see an animal that is the symbol of the United States. Follow the path that has **long e** words to find out which animal it is.

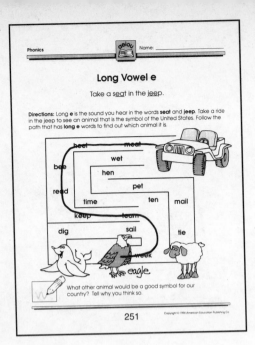

beet   meat

bee   wet

read   hen

time   pet   ten   mail

keep   team

dig   sail   tie

week

eagle

What other animal would be a good symbol for our country? Tell why you think so.

251

Long Vowels

Directions: Read the words in the box. Use the words to find the name of each picture. Write the name on the line.

rain	soap	seal	mail	toad	meat

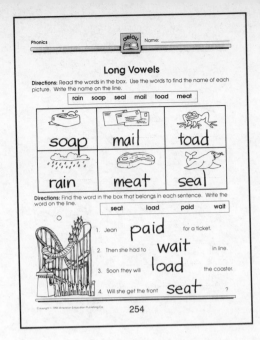

| soap | mail | toad |
| rain | meat | seal |

Directions: Find the word in the box that belongs in each sentence. Write the word on the line.

seat	load	paid	wait

1. Jean **paid** for a ticket.
2. Then she had to **wait** in line.
3. Soon they will **load** the coaster.
4. Will she get the front **seat** ?

254

Exploring Short and Long Vowels

cap + e = cape

Directions: Adding **e** to the end of the short vowel word **cap** changes it to the long vowel word **cape.** Cut out the tub and the water. Cut on the dotted lines to make slits. Slip the water through the slits in the tub. Next, cut out the tube. Paste the tube in the tub, but don't paste the cap down.

When the cap is on the tube, read the short vowel word. Then, fold the cap back to show the **e.** Read the long vowel word.

Diagram:

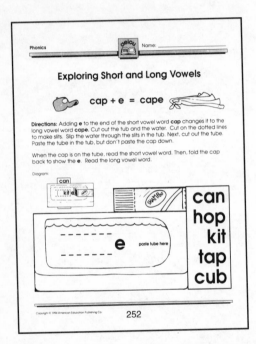

can
hop
kit
tap
cub

e   paste tube here

252

A Plan for Reading

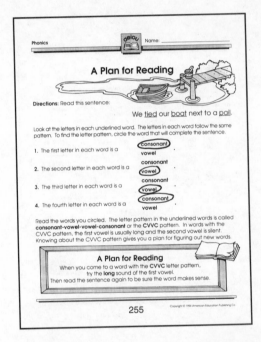

Directions: Read this sentence:

We tied our boat next to a pail.

Look at the letters in each underlined word. The letters in each word follow the same pattern. To find the letter pattern, circle the word that will complete the sentence.

1. The first letter in each word is a   (**consonant**) / vowel
2. The second letter in each word is a   (**vowel**) / consonant
3. The third letter in each word is a   (**vowel**) / consonant
4. The fourth letter in each word is a   (**consonant**) / vowel

Read the words you circled. The letter pattern in the underlined words is called **consonant-vowel-vowel-consonant** or the **CVVC** pattern. In words with the CVVC pattern, the first vowel is usually long and the second vowel is silent. Knowing about the CVVC pattern gives you a plan for figuring out new words.

> **A Plan for Reading**
> When you come to a word with the **CVVC** letter pattern,
> try the **long** sound of the first vowel.
> Then read the sentence again to be sure the word makes sense.

255

A Plan for Reading

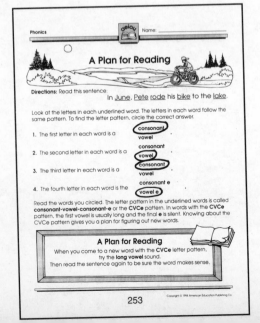

Directions: Read this sentence: In June, Pete rode his bike to the lake.

Look at the letters in each underlined word. The letters in each word follow the same pattern. To find the letter pattern, circle the correct answer.

1. The first letter in each word is a   (**consonant**) / vowel
2. The second letter in each word is a   (**vowel**) / consonant
3. The third letter in each word is a   (**consonant**) / vowel
4. The fourth letter in each word is the   (**vowel e**) / consonant e

Read the words you circled. The letter pattern in the underlined words is called **consonant-vowel-consonant-e** or the **CVCe** pattern. In words with the **CVCe** pattern, the first vowel is usually long and the final **e** is silent. Knowing about the CVCe pattern gives you a plan for figuring out new words.

> **A Plan for Reading**
> When you come to a new word with the **CVCe** letter pattern,
> try the **long vowel** sound.
> Then read the sentence again to be sure the word makes sense.

253

Review Long Vowels

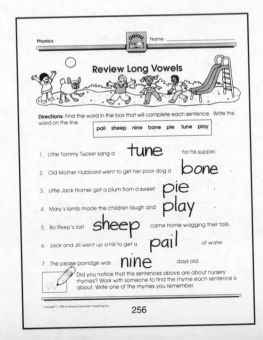

Directions: Find the word in the box that will complete each sentence. Write the word on the line.

pail	sheep	nine	bone	pie	tune	play

1. Little Tommy Tucker sang a **tune** for his supper.
2. Old Mother Hubbard went to get her poor dog a **bone**
3. Little Jack Horner got a plum from a sweet **pie**
4. Mary's lamb made the children laugh and **play** .
5. Bo Peep's lost **sheep** came home wagging their tails.
6. Jack and Jill went up a hill to get a **pail** of water.
7. The pease porridge was **nine** days old.

Did you notice that the sentences above are about nursery rhymes? Work with someone to find the rhyme each sentence is about. Write one of the rhymes you remember.

256

348

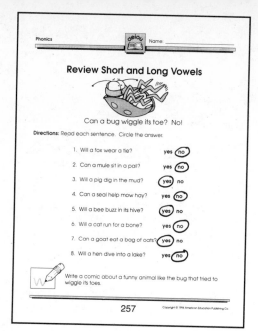

Phonics — Name: _____

Review Short and Long Vowels

Can a bug wiggle its toe? No!

Directions: Read each sentence. Circle the answer.

1. Will a fox wear a tie? — yes (no)
2. Can a mule sit in a pail? — yes (no)
3. Will a pig dig in the mud? — (yes) no
4. Can a seal help mow hay? — yes (no)
5. Will a bee buzz in its hive? — (yes) no
6. Will a cat run for a bone? — yes (no)
7. Can a goat eat a bag of oats? — (yes) no
8. Will a hen dive into a lake? — yes (no)

Write a comic about a funny animal like the bug that tried to wiggle its toes.

257

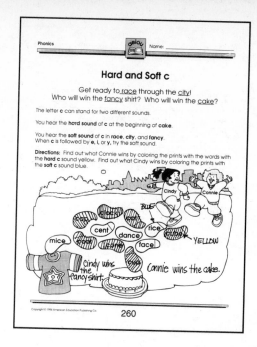

Phonics — Name: _____

Hard and Soft c

Get ready to <u>race</u> through the <u>city</u>!
Who will win the <u>fancy</u> shirt? Who will win the <u>cake</u>?

The letter **c** can stand for two different sounds.

You hear the **hard sound** of c at the beginning of **cake**.

You hear the **soft sound** of c in **race**, **city**, and **fancy**.
When **c** is followed by **e**, **i**, or **y**, try the soft sound.

Directions: Find out what Connie wins by coloring the prints with the words with the **hard c** sound yellow. Find out what Cindy wins by coloring the prints with the **soft c** sound blue.

260

Phonics — Name: _____

Final y as a Vowel

Our puppy stays dr<u>y</u> in the <u>yard</u>.

You know that **y** is a consonant. When **y** is at the beginning of a word, it stands for the sound at the beginning of **yard**.

Did you know that **y** can be a vowel too?

Sometimes **y** can stand for the **long e** sound at the end of **puppy**. Try this sound when **y** is the only vowel at the end of a word with more than one syllable or part.

Sometimes **y** can stand for the **long i** sound at the end of **dry**. Try this sound when **y** is the only vowel at the end of a one syllable word.

Directions: Say each picture name. Circle the word that names the picture. If **y** stands for the **long e** sound in **puppy**, color the picture **brown**. If **y** stands for the **long i** sound in **dry**, color the picture **orange**.

258

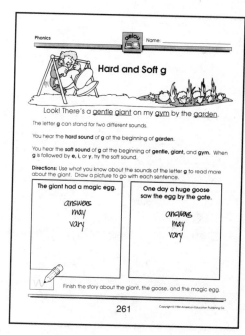

Phonics — Name: _____

Hard and Soft g

Look! There's a <u>gentle</u> <u>giant</u> on my <u>gym</u> by the <u>garden</u>.

The letter **g** can stand for two different sounds.

You hear the **hard sound** of g at the beginning of **garden**.

You hear the **soft sound** of g at the beginning of **gentle**, **giant**, and **gym**. When **g** is followed by **e**, **i**, or **y**, try the soft sound.

Directions: Use what you know about the sounds of the letter **g** to read more about the giant. Draw a picture to go with each sentence.

The giant had a magic egg.	One day a huge goose saw the egg by the gate.
answers may vary	answers may vary

Finish the story about the giant, the goose, and the magic egg.

261

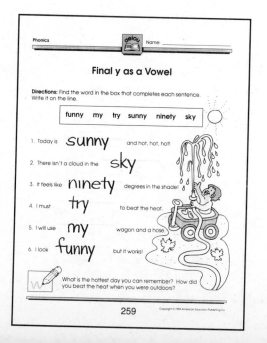

Phonics — Name: _____

Final y as a Vowel

Directions: Find the word in the box that completes each sentence. Write it on the line.

funny	my	try	sunny	ninety	sky

1. Today is **sunny** and hot, hot, hot!
2. There isn't a cloud in the **sky**
3. It feels like **ninety** degrees in the shade!
4. I must **try** to beat the heat.
5. I will use **my** wagon and a hose.
6. I look **funny** but it works!

What is the hottest day you can remember? How did you beat the heat when you were outdoors?

259

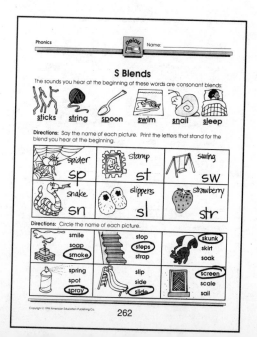

Phonics — Name: _____

S Blends

The sounds you hear at the beginning of these words are consonant blends:

<u>st</u>icks <u>str</u>ing <u>sp</u>oon <u>sw</u>im <u>sn</u>ail <u>sl</u>eep

Directions: Say the name of each picture. Print the letters that stand for the blend you hear at the beginning.

spider **sp**	stamp **st**	swing **sw**
snake **sn**	slippers **sl**	strawberry **str**

Directions: Circle the name of each picture.

smile / soap / (smoke)	stop / (steps) / strap	(skunk) / skirt / soak
spring / spot / (spray)	slip / side / (slide)	(screen) / scale / sail

262

349

S Blends

Directions: Read the words in the box. Then look at the picture. Use the words in the box to label the picture. The first one shows you what to do.

| snow | scarf | sweater | skates | sled | squirrel |

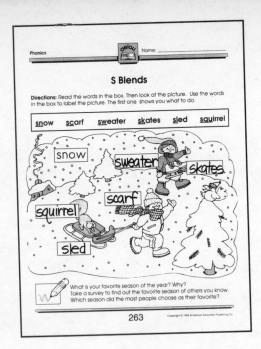

What is your favorite season of the year? Why? Take a survey to find out the favorite season of others you know. Which season did the most people choose as their favorite?

263

R Blends

Read each word. Listen for the blend at the beginning of each word.

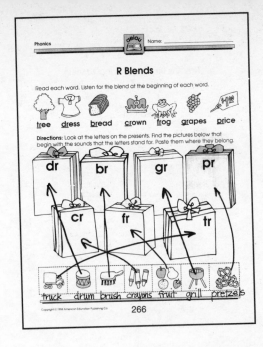

tree   dress   bread   crown   frog   grapes   price

Directions: Look at the letters on the presents. Find the pictures below that begin with the sounds that the letters stand for. Paste them where they belong.

dr   br   gr   pr

cr   fr   tr

truck   drum   brush   crayons   fruit   grill   pretzels

266

L Blends

Directions:

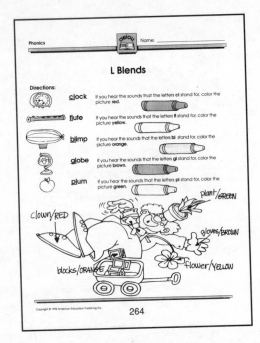

clock — If you hear the sounds that the letters **cl** stand for, color the picture **red**.

flute — If you hear the sounds that the letters **fl** stand for, color the picture **yellow**.

blimp — If you hear the sounds that the letters **bl** stand for, color the picture **orange**.

globe — If you hear the sounds that the letters **gl** stand for, color the picture **brown**.

plum — If you hear the sounds that the letters **pl** stand for, color the picture **green**.

plant/GREEN
clown/RED
gloves/BROWN
blocks/ORANGE
flower/YELLOW

264

R Blends

Directions: Use each word in the box to complete the puzzle.

| brick | drain | crab | train | prize |

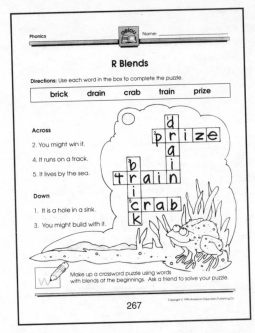

Across

2. You might win it.

4. It runs on a track.

5. It lives by the sea.

Down

1. It is a hole in a sink.

3. You might build with it.

prize
drain
brick
train
crab

Make up a crossword puzzle using words with blends at the beginnings. Ask a friend to solve your puzzle.

267

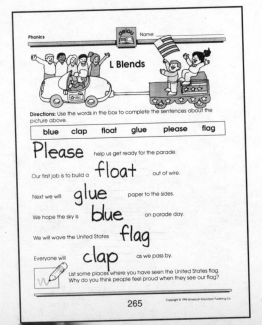

L Blends

Directions: Use the words in the box to complete the sentences about the picture above.

| blue | clap | float | glue | please | flag |

Please help us get ready for the parade.

Our first job is to build a **float** out of wire.

Next we will **glue** paper to the sides.

We hope the sky is **blue** on parade day.

We will wave the United States **flag**

Everyone will **clap** as we pass by.

List some places where you have seen the United States flag. Why do you think people feel proud when they see our flag?

265

Exploring Consonant Blends

Directions: Cut out the train and the smoke. Cut on the dotted lines to make slits. Slip the smoke through the slits on the train. Slide the smoke and read each new word.

Diagram:

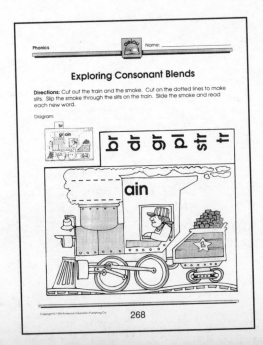

br   dr   gr   pl   str   tr

ain

268

Review Consonant Blends

Directions: Read each sentence. Circle the word that completes each sentence. Write the word on the line.

1. I like to sit and **dream** about what I want to be.   (dream / stream / clean)

2. I might let drivers know when to **stop** .   (fry / plant / stop)

3. I could teach children to read and **spell** .   (sleep / spell / smell)

4. It would be fun to own a **store** .   (store / step / flame)

5. Maybe I will be a big movie **star** .   (plant / dress / star)

6. That dream really makes me **smile** !   (smile / grill / small)

What do you dream you might do someday?

269

Final Consonant Digraphs

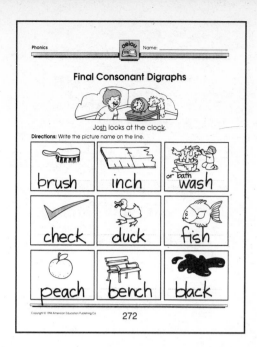

Jo**sh** looks at the clo**ck**.

Directions: Write the picture name on the line.

brush	inch	wash
check	duck	fish
peach	bench	black

272

Beginning Consonant Digraphs

Let's visit the **chicks** and **sheep** at the petting farm.

chicks   **sheep**

The letters you see at the beginning of the words **chicks** and **sheep** are called consonant digraphs. The two consonants go together to stand for one sound.

Directions: Cut out the pictures at the bottom. Say each picture name. If the picture name begins with the same sound as **chicks**, paste it near the chicks. If the picture name begins with the same sound as **sheep**, paste it near the sheep.

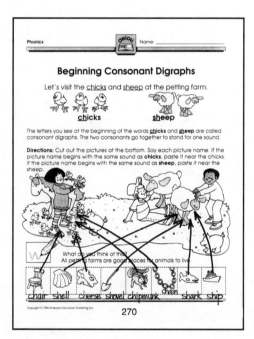

What do you think of this?
All petting farms are good places for animals to live.

chair   shell   cheese   shovel   chipmunk   chain   shark   ship

270

A Plan for Reading

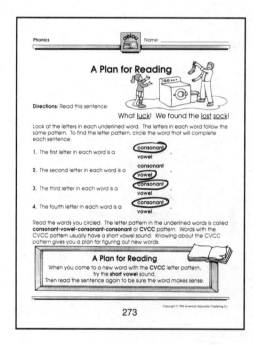

Directions: Read this sentence.

What **luck**! We found the **lost sock**!

Look at the letters in each underlined word. The letters in each word follow the same pattern. To find the letter pattern, circle the word that will complete each sentence.

1. The first letter in each word is a   (**consonant** / vowel)

2. The second letter in each word is a   (consonant / **vowel**)

3. The third letter in each word is a   (**consonant** / vowel).

4. The fourth letter in each word is a   (**consonant** / vowel)

Read the words you circled. The letter pattern in the underlined words is called **consonant-vowel-consonant-consonant** or **CVCC** pattern. Words with the CVCC pattern usually have a short vowel sound. Knowing about the CVCC pattern gives you a plan for figuring out new words.

A Plan for Reading

When you come to a new word with the **CVCC** letter pattern, try the **short vowel** sound.
Then read the sentence again to be sure the word makes sense.

273

Beginning Consonant Digraphs

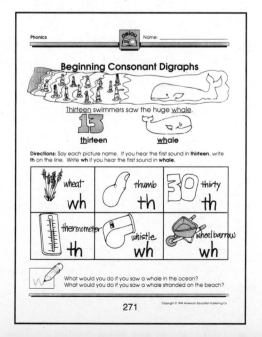

Thirteen swimmers saw the huge **whale**.

thirteen   **whale**

Directions: Say each picture name. If you hear the first sound in **thirteen**, write **th** on the line. Write **wh** if you hear the first sound in **whale**.

wheat — wh	thumb — th	thirty — th
thermometer — th	whistle — wh	wheelbarrow — wh

What would you do if you saw a whale in the ocean?
What would you do if you saw a whale stranded on the beach?

271

Review Consonant Digraphs

Directions: Read the words in the box. Then look at the picture. Use the words in the box to label the picture. The first one shows you what to do.

chimney	shed	wheel	thimble
shoes	path	rock	

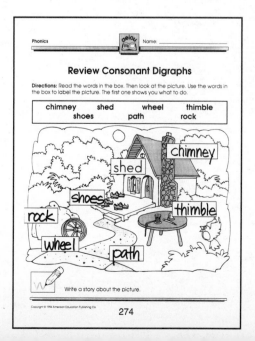

chimney   shed   shoes   rock   wheel   thimble   path

Write a story about the picture.

274

351

Review Your Plans for Reading

Directions: Write the underlined words under the correct letter pattern. The first one shows you what to do.

Tom began to moan. "It will take me a long time to read this good book. I'd like to be able to read all the words by myself. I can't wait to see what happens next!"

"You can do it," Mr. Jet reminded him. "There are many ways to figure out new words on your own. One way is to look for letter patterns."

CVC	CVCC	CVCe	CVVC
Tom	will	take	moan
can	long	time	read
Jet	next	like	wait

What do you think of this?
Phonics can help me be a better reader and speller.

275　Copyright © 1994 American Education Publishing Co.

Use Your Plans for Reading

Directions: Write the words on the books above the correct letter pattern on the bookmark. Cut out the bookmark. Fold the bookmark on the dotted line and tape the sides. As you read, use the bookmark to help you remember the four plans for figuring out new words.

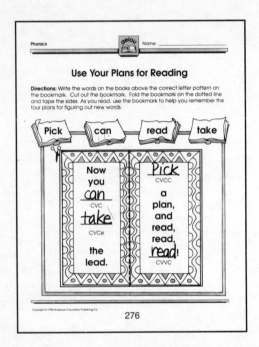

Pick　can　read　take

Now you **can**
CVC
take
CVCe
the lead.

Pick
CVCC
a plan, and read, read, **read**!
CVVC

276